THE JUNCTURE CODE

A **Leader's Playbook** for Navigating Change and Growth

DAVID L ZIMMERMAN, MSC, CPC

Editing, design, distribution by Bublish
Published by AMAXXA Press

ISBN: 978-1-647049-39-3 (paperback)
ISBN: 978-1-647049-33-1 (hardcover)
ISBN: 978-1-647049-31-7 (eBook)
ISBN: 978-1-647049-34-8 (audiobook)

CONTENTS

INTRODUCTION

THE ELEVATOR DOORS slid open with a pleasant chime, revealing the dimly lit executive floor of Wells Fargo's regional headquarters in downtown Los Angeles. I took a deep breath, stepping into the dark and silence, my heart thudding in my chest.

It was just before 6:30 a.m. in 2003, and I needed to be at my desk early to monitor the markets, which were about to open in New York. It was also my first day on the job. My steps echoed loudly on the marble floor as I strode past empty cubicles and polished conference room windows, making my way down a long and elegant hall. Finally, I came upon a heavy wooden door with my name engraved on a small brass plate in the middle.

What the hell have I done? I thought as I turned the knob with a sweaty palm.

As the new Chief of Staff, I would be managing seven directors responsible for nearly five hundred team members. I'd always enjoyed the challenge of change, but this was the biggest I'd faced in my career. I'd left everything familiar and comfortable behind after departing my role as the Director of Financial Advisor Professional Development at Prudential Securities in New York. I'd always been on the investment side of finance, but was officially moving to the banking side—and it was a whole different animal. If that weren't intimidating enough, I was making this career shift in one of Wells Fargo's largest regions, with more than three hundred branches.

Despite my initial reluctance, I knew this was a great professional opportunity and the right move for me and my wife, Debbie. She had family in California, and we would need them nearby to support us through her illness. It was a difficult time, and this opportunity presented a literal lifeline. Debbie's illness was already a constant strain—physically, emotionally, and spiritually. Watching someone you love fight for their life drains you in ways that most people never see or understand. It's hard to show up with clarity and strength at work when your world at home is filled with fear, uncertainty, and fragile hope. Having her family nearby in California gave us support we hadn't even known we'd need: someone to sit with her, help with meals, or simply be present when I couldn't be. That support allowed me to focus when I needed to lead others, even when my heart was somewhere else.

The truth is that our personal junctures don't stop at the office door. They shape how we show up—what energy we have, how clear our thinking is, how patient or reactive we become. And yet, most people at work don't know we're carrying those personal burdens. We're expected to lead, perform, and decide as if our personal world isn't pulling at us. That was precisely why this move, as daunting as it was professionally, was a stabilizing force personally. It reminded me that the junctures we face at home often have a deeper influence on

     DAVID L ZIMMERMAN, MSC, CPC

our professional choices than we acknowledge and that both need to be navigated with care, support, and intentionality.

That early morning in downtown Los Angeles wasn't just the beginning of a new job—it was the beginning of learning how to lead through both visible and invisible pressure. Standing alone in my new office, I tried not to be intimidated by the dozen ornately framed, smiling portraits of the people who had held this position before me. Surely they would soon sit in judgment of me.

Am I even ready for this kind of role? I fretted.

I settled into the top-grain leather chair behind my expansive, solid-mahogany desk and spread my open palms out over the polished surface of it. "You are *way* out of your league here, sir," I whispered to myself, using a sleeve to buff out my freshly-made fingerprints.

With another deep breath, I stared out the floor-to-ceiling window to my right, observing the city twinkling twelve stories below. It was slowly coming to life at the first signs of dawn. I leaned back and tried to steady my nerves. *Leadership,* I reminded myself, *isn't about having all the answers all the time. It's about having the courage, clarity, stamina, openness, and integrity to learn on your feet and face all the questions, uncertainties, and challenges head on. You've navigated plenty of change before. You know how to do this. Just take it one step at a time. It's just another juncture—a big one, yes—but you've got this.*

At the time, I had no idea that my wife would only be with me for one more year, and that I would remain with Wells Fargo in various capacities for thirteen. I had no idea that my team at Wells Fargo would help me, along with my family, through the aftermath of losing her. Despite my initial fears, I have never regretted moving to California, personally or professionally.

But that's the thing about life—it's filled with transitions, challenges, losses, and opportunities, some of which are thrust upon us and others which are offered to us. Either way, we have to navigate each, because there is no pause button when life gets tough or confusing. Challenges and opportunities come and go. They are not what defines us. It's what we do in each situation that changes the trajectory of our lives. As Albert Camus so poignantly said, "Life is indeed a sum of all our choices." That is why it's best to face each juncture—the good, bad, and the ugly—from a position of strength.

Perhaps you too have faced decisions and crossroads so challenging they consumed your every waking moment, leaving you emotionally drained and mentally exhausted. Whether it was a career-defining choice, a deeply personal decision, or a pivotal leadership moment, life's junctures carry an invisible weight that pulls at every thread of our being. Fear, anxiety, guilt, and doubt often make it more difficult to find the clarity and confidence needed to make good decisions or forge new paths. Though these emotions may seem like obstacles, they are actually signals, reminders that our values, perspectives, and responsibilities are part of the equation as we weigh our options.

Looking back over my thirty-plus years in leadership, I still vividly remember many of the junctures I have faced—like the one I shared above. Sometimes I nailed the situation; other times things went a bit sideways. Either way, I kept learning. Some of my decisions were grounded in careful, dispassionate analysis while others were reactionary, even impulsive. Having struggled through my fair share of restless nights, swirling what-ifs, and inner tug-of-wars as I faced big decisions and hard choices, I came to accept friction as a crucial part of the

   DAVID L ZIMMERMAN, MSC, CPC

journey. It took years, but I finally understood that this is how we work through our personal values, priorities, and even fears in relation to what is put in front of us. Yes, each juncture carries its own unique lessons—but beyond that, patterns emerge. Every decision I made influenced how I navigated the next juncture, often in ways I didn't fully understand. Over time, there was also a powerful compounding effect that strengthened, even transformed, my decision-making skills and process. Having coached hundreds of leaders and professionals, each grappling with their own unique challenges and opportunities, I have come to realize that making choices and dealing with change is not about the absence of doubt or fear, but about the way in which we respond to them. Every juncture offers us an opportunity to pause, recalibrate, and move forward with greater intention and focus.

As my decision-making skills evolved as a leader, I often wished I could revisit certain past junctures and do things differently. Of course, hindsight is 20/20 and reality doesn't afford us the luxury of rewinding the clock. But I wanted to do something constructive with everything I had learned and experienced. This led me to build a framework for myself and my clients, a way to approach critical junctures with more clarity and confidence. Too often the competing priorities and pressures of leadership cause us to move through the decision-making process quickly when we should be taking time to pause, reflect, or recognize the weight of each decision. We all need to be more intentional, consistent, and structured in our approach. We need a framework, a code, to help us slow down and assess the broader picture.

The Juncture Code was born from this intention. Designed not only to help you effectively navigate the professional decisions and junctures in your life, this book can also help you become more cognizant of the science, experiences, and influences that shape your decision-making process. In addition to sharing my many years of leadership and coaching experience and stories, I've also done in-depth research on the topic, tapping into more than 150 expert sources. Organized into two sections, this book is a call to approach every decision with the intentionality, adaptability, and resilience it deserves in order to lead from a place of alignment, strength, and consistency. *The Juncture Code* is your companion on that journey.

Understand How You and Your Brain Work

Chapters 1–9 of *The Juncture Code* delve into the psychological, physiological, and social dynamics that underpin our decision-making processes as humans. These foundational chapters provide insight into the less visible forces that influence our choices. The goal is to help you develop the self-awareness necessary to navigate critical junctures effectively. Together, these chapters lay the groundwork for a more structured approach to leadership, one where you can move from self-awareness to intentional action.

Learn the Juncture Code

Chapters 10–15 dive into the steps and framework that make up the Juncture Code. Each chapter in this section focuses on one step, providing practical tools and actionable strategies to navigate complex situations.

Design Your Personal Code

Chapter 16 explores how to use the Juncture Code to develop your own personal code. It invites leaders to turn each step into actions that resonate with their unique values, goals, and circumstances. By the end, you will have a code that is both adaptable

    DAVID L ZIMMERMAN, MSC, CPC

and deeply personal. Leadership is never static; it is a journey that demands constant evolution. This means you'll need to adapt your personal code over time. Each new challenge and experience offers a chance to refine your understanding and approach, allowing your decision-making process to evolve throughout your career.

At the end of each chapter, you will find:

Key takeaways to reinforce the important points explored in each chapter.

Case studies that demonstrate the principles explored in each chapter.

Reflections to deepen your self-awareness, clarify your values, and translate insights into actionable growth.

Self-audits to help you evaluate where you stand today and identify areas for growth. These audits are designed to guide you toward deeper reflection. Be as honest as possible in assessing yourself. It will help you uncover where you excel and where you have room to grow.

Exercises to help you turn what you have learned into an action plan for personal and professional growth. Many of these exercises have a writing or documentation component, so you might want to dedicate a notebook or journal to these exercises.

Life has always been filled with junctures, but with the accelerating rate of change the world is experiencing and the growing abundance of choices we have as professionals, I felt now, more than ever, the world needed *The Juncture Code*. At its core, this book is a blueprint for navigating life's critical decisions and moments. It offers a comprehensive, customizable, and actionable framework that recognizes leadership as a deeply personal journey shaped by key decisions and transitions.

And I want you to know this: I didn't write this from a safe distance. The stories that open each chapter aren't polished parables, they're my real life—times I was in over my head, unsure, sometimes scared, and occasionally wrong. They come from seasons when I tried to lead while grieving, doubting, or simply holding things together at home. There are wins I'm proud of and mistakes I'd handle differently if I could. I have chosen to share these stories because I want you know you're not alone when leadership feels heavy and complicated. You're not the only one who questions yourself before walking into a room or lies awake reliving decisions you can't undo. You're not the only one trying to be strong for others while feeling fragile yourself.

I hope *The Juncture Code* helps you grow into the leader you wish to become. To your growth and success!—David

     DAVID L ZIMMERMAN, MSC, CPC

CHAPTER 1

A FOUNDATION FOR STRONG LEADERSHIP

"The growth and development of people is the highest calling of leadership."

—Harvey Firestone

HAVE YOU EVER questioned your ability to handle the constant demands of leadership? Maybe you've wondered if you're truly equipped to navigate the unexpected challenges, endless decision-making, and pressure to make the right call when the stakes feel impossibly high. If so, you're not alone. I've faced these doubts often in my career. But effective leadership isn't about having all the right answers or never making mistakes. It's about cultivating the mental strength to embrace uncertainty with clarity and purpose.

Every leader faces difficulties, but the best develop the adaptability and resilience necessary to get through the rough patches and arrive at their intended destination feeling empowered rather than weakened by the experience. When a leader can demonstrate adaptability and resilience, their teams not only survive—they thrive. These qualities are crucial for high-performing leaders, teams, and companies. For me, this realization was a turning point in my leadership journey—and it's why this book begins with a call to build a strong cognitive foundation grounded in adaptability and resilience.

Let's start with **cognitive adaptability:** the ability to adjust one's thinking and problem-solving strategies in the face of pressure, change, or uncertainty. Leaders who learn cognitive adaptability can process complex information and recalibrate even as the ground continues to shift beneath their feet. This type of mental agility allows them to strike a productive balance between logic and intuition when a fluid situation requires both. Research shows that leaders who develop cognitive adaptability are far better prepared to successfully steer their teams through tough times and capitalize on opportunities.[1] Cognitive resilience, on the other hand, is the ability to maintain your wellbeing and recover despite the continuous challenges and stress of your job. It's what gives you the stamina to keep leading effectively over time.

We are not born with either cognitive adaptability or resilience. They are disciplines we must learn and practice. Like exercising our muscles, cognitive adaptability and resilience are strengthened through use. They are core leadership skills that you should work on every day so you are ready when the

---

[1]   Goleman, D., Boyatzis, R., & McKee, A. (2013). Primal leadership: Unleashing the power of emotional intelligence. Harvard Business Review Press.

    DAVID L ZIMMERMAN, MSC, CPC

next challenge hits, which it inevitably will. When you commit to learning these crucial skills, you become better equipped to cut through the noise, keep your emotions in check, prioritize efficiently, and zero in on what really matters.

In a world that is changing faster by the day, leaders who can think on their feet, adapt quickly, make effective decisions amid changing circumstances, and continue doing it for the long-term have a significant edge on those who cannot. Cognitive adaptability and resilience create the foundation you need to lead in the twenty-first century. These are no longer just nice-to-have "soft skills." They are essential modern leadership skills that create a significant competitive advantage for you, your team, and your organization. Drawing from developmental psychology, behavioral science, and real-world insights, let's explore a few other key disciplines you need to learn and adopt to create a cognitive foundation strong enough to support the weight of modern leadership and decision-making.

THE THREE DISCIPLINES OF COGNITIVE ADAPTABILITY

Every day, leaders are bombarded with massive amounts of information—and let's be honest, much of it is not useful, relevant, or credible. Effective leaders know how to ignore the noise and focus on what matters most to achieve their goals. Cognitive adaptability, as mentioned, is a core discipline that gives you the tools you need to become an effective leader. It is built on three important subdisciplines. Here's a quick overview of them:

> **Cognitive Clarity**
> Before you can adapt to a situation, you need to understand it. This means being aware of more than just the facts. Cognitive clarity is about being fully present. It's about tapping into a mental state

where your thoughts are organized and focused, enabling you to effectively process, analyze, and act on the right information at the right time and in the right order. Think of it as your leadership GPS. It keeps you alert and headed in the right direction. In order to achieve and sustain cognitive clarity, you must take care of your mind, body, and spirit. Healthy sleep, exercise, and eating habits all come into play, as does **mindfulness**: the practice of being fully present in the moment and observing without judgment.

Emotional Regulation

Ever feel your blood pressure spike in a high-stakes meeting? That's your amygdala, your brain's fight-or-flight center, kicking into gear. This evolutionary mechanism, which once kept us safe from wild animals and other threats, can become a big problem in the modern boardroom, if left unchecked. When our fight-or-flight mechanism is triggered, we are led by our emotions and clear thinking goes out the window. **Emotional regulation** requires self-awareness and understanding of our triggers. Once these are in place, practices can be developed to modulate reactions and responses. It's not about ignoring your emotions—it's about managing them, so they don't derail you. Research shows that leaders who can regulate their emotions effectively are better decision-makers and more trusted by their teams.[2] The next time you're feeling overwhelmed or triggered, take a step back and ask yourself, "What's

---

[2] Gross, J. J. (2015). Emotion regulation: Current status and future prospects. Psychological Inquiry, 26(1), 1–26. https://doi.org/10.1080/1047840X.2014.940781

 DAVID L ZIMMERMAN, MSC, CPC

the most constructive way to respond here?" We'll dive deeper into this topic later in the book.

Adaptive Problem-Solving

The third discipline is **adaptive problem-solving:** the ability to stay open to new solutions when things don't go as planned, as is so often the case. Adaptive problem-solving is about seeing challenges from multiple angles, questioning assumptions and biases (even and perhaps especially your own), and considering new ideas with an open mind. A flexible approach is especially important when you're dealing with complex or evolving situations. If you hit a roadblock, how quickly are you able to overcome it or pivot to a new path forward? Like the other two disciplines of cognitive adaptability, you cannot just call upon this type of positive behavior in the middle of a crisis—it must be learned and practiced every day.

COGNITIVE RESILIENCE AND SELF-CARE

Even the most adaptable leaders have bad days and tough quarters. Mistakes are made, deals are lost, and surprises happen. That's when cognitive resilience gets you through. Heck, even when things are going well, leaders need stamina to face the grueling pace of business. This is where lifestyle habits play a role. Do you get enough sleep, eat well, and exercise regularly? Have you developed healthy coping mechanisms to deal with the stress of your position? Do you make time for personal growth in addition to professional growth? Do you have a healthy home life and social life? If you have answered "no" to any of these questions, there is work to be done. You cannot neglect self-care as a leader. The job is too tough, and the personal and professional stakes are too high.

THE ROLE OF CORE VALUES

Let's talk about how to stay grounded as a leader when everything seems uncertain. **Core values** are what keep a leader steady in tough times. They are based on one's fundamental beliefs about what is important, right, and desirable in their personal and professional lives—think honesty, integrity, empathy, respect, and other aspects that define a moral compass. Understanding your core values will offer the sort of stability you need to make decisions and choices with confidence and clarity. Understanding your core values enhances your cognitive adaptability and resilience because it ensures that your decisions align with what truly matters to you. Instead of being swayed by immediate pressures or external noise, leaders who stay true to their core values make decisions that they are less likely to regret. This creates consistency and builds trust. Imagine you're facing a tough strategic decision, like whether to enter a new market or pivot your team's priorities. Without core values, it's easy to get caught up in the short-term risks or conflicting opinions. Your core values help you weigh all options through a reliable lens. This not only simplifies decision-making but also ensures that your actions stay true to who you are and what you believe as a leader.

KEY TAKEAWAYS

The best leaders are not defined by an unbroken string of perfect choices—they are defined by how they think when choices are hard. Cognitive clarity, emotional regulation, and adaptive problemsolving give you a repeatable framework for cutting through noise and acting with intent. Pair that framework with cognitive resilience; the commitment to rest, reflect, and clue into selfcare, and you will keep your mind sharp. This is a solid foundation for leadership in the age of relentless change and nonstop disruption. But when the unexpected happens

 DAVID L ZIMMERMAN, MSC, CPC

and you must make a snap decision under pressure, that is when understanding your core values will pay off dramatically. Not only will they ensure that your decisions align with who you want to be professionally, but they will ensure that your decisions align with who you want to be *personally*.

A leader who acts with a clear set of values can pivot without drifting, adjust without losing credibility, and inspire their teams to follow even when the path forward is uncertain. Developing these capabilities is not a oneoff exercise; it is daily, deliberate practice, and a discipline that you develop intentionally over time. Each meeting is a chance to refine cognitive clarity. Each moment of tension is a rehearsal in emotional regulation. Each unexpected obstacle is an invitation to flex adaptive problemsolving. And every evening's winddown routine, workout, or quiet walk is a small investment in the resilience you will need to do it all again tomorrow. Leadership excellence is built in these ordinary, easily bypassed disciplines. Start now, stay consistent, and you will lead not only with confidence, but with the calm conviction that you can meet whatever the world throws at you.

- Cognitive adaptability and resilience are key disciplines that serve as the cornerstones of effective leadership. Together, they allow leaders to successfully navigate complex, uncertain environments on an ongoing basis.

- Cognitive adaptability is built on three sub-disciplines: cognitive clarity, emotional regulation, and adaptive problem-solving.

- Cognitive resilience requires self-awareness and self-care; both are key to effective leadership.

- Establishing a clear understanding of your core values will lead to making confident and informed decisions that align with your beliefs. This not only enhances adaptability but also builds trust.

CASE STUDY: LINCOLN'S CORE VALUES, ADAPTABILITY, AND RESILIENCE

President Abraham Lincoln's path to leadership was unconventional. He didn't come from privilege, and his education consisted primarily of self-directed learning. Yet his intellectual curiosity and moral clarity allowed him to develop a cognitive foundation that would sustain him through one of the most turbulent periods in American history.[3] His core values, formed through personal hardships and deep empathy, gave him the resilience to confront some of the nation's most polarizing issues, such as slavery and the preservation of the Union.[4]

Lincoln's core values complemented his cognitive adaptability and resilience. For example, his decision to issue the Emancipation Proclamation in 1863 reflected his unwavering belief in justice and equality while balancing the political necessity of maintaining support from border states.[5] His steady leadership during the chaos of the Civil War demonstrated a remarkable ability to adapt without compromising his principles. Whether dealing with setbacks on the battlefield or opposition within his own government, Lincoln's decisions were consistently aligned with his core values.[6]

Modern leadership scholars echo the importance of this kind of values-driven resilience. Authors and leadership experts, James

---

[3] Donald, D. H. (1996). Lincoln. Simon & Schuster.

[4] Guelzo, A. C. (2000). Abraham Lincoln: Redeemer president. Wm. B. Eerdmans Publishing Co.

[5] Foner, E. (2010). The fiery trial: Abraham Lincoln and American slavery. W. W. Norton & Company.

[6] Kearns Goodwin, D. (2005). *Team of rivals: The political genius of Abraham Lincoln*. Simon & Schuster.

 DAVID L ZIMMERMAN, MSC, CPC

Kouzes and Barry Posner, who wrote the bestselling book *The Leadership Challenge*, emphasize that leaders who ground their decisions in deeply held beliefs are better equipped to navigate turbulence and uncertainty.[7] "Values serve as a stabilizing force in turbulent times," they write, "helping leaders to hold true to a vision, even when the journey is difficult. Lincoln epitomized this, using his values as a guide to ensure that even in the darkest times, his work remained principled and focused. His legendary style offers timeless lessons for navigating complexity and adversity. By studying his journey, leaders can uncover practical strategies for anchoring their commitment to core values, remaining adaptable and resilient in the face of adversity, and fostering meaningful change through reflection and collaboration.

REFLECTION

Ask yourself the following questions and write your answers in your journal. After, take time to reflect on your discoveries.

1. What experiences have shaped your leadership values?

2. Which core values anchor your decision-making?

3. How often do you challenge yourself to grow cognitively every day?

4. What practices strengthen your resilience in tough times?

5. How do you adapt your leadership based on new insights?

---

[7] Kouzes, J. M., & Posner, B. Z. (2017). *The leadership challenge: How to make extraordinary things happen in organizations* (6th ed.). Jossey-Bass.

SELF-AUDIT

Rate yourself on a scale from one to ten, where one means "rarely or not at all" and ten means "frequently or very well."

1. I actively pursue learning opportunities to expand my leadership perspective.

   1 2 3 4 5 6 7 8 9 10

2. I regularly engage with diverse viewpoints to challenge my assumptions.

   1 2 3 4 5 6 7 8 9 10

3. I reflect on past decisions to refine my approach to leadership.

   1 2 3 4 5 6 7 8 9 10

4. I have identified core values that guide my decisions.

   1 2 3 4 5 6 7 8 9 10

5. I am adaptable, adjusting my strategies based on new information.

   1 2 3 4 5 6 7 8 9 10

6. I balance my core values with strategic flexibility.

   1 2 3 4 5 6 7 8 9 10

7. I understand the importance of continuous cognitive growth in leadership.

   1 2 3 4 5 6 7 8 9 10

8. I actively seek challenges that promote cognitive adaptability.

   1 2 3 4 5 6 7 8 9 10

9. I approach difficult decisions with mental clarity and resilience.

   1 2 3 4 5 6 7 8 9 10

10. I am committed to building a foundation of cognitive growth.

1   2   3   4   5   6   7   8   9   10

EXERCISE: DISCOVER YOUR COGNITIVE FOUNDATION

Let's explore your core values. This isn't simply a reflection—it's about creating a deliberate and actionable connection between your core values and your leadership decisions. By revisiting past challenges, you'll uncover the principles that guide you and reinforce your ability to navigate future complexities with clarity and confidence.

1. Describe a Defining Leadership Moment
   Think back to a moment when you faced a significant challenge as a leader. What was at stake? What emotions did you feel? Write down everything you remember about this situation; the context, the decisions you made, and the outcomes.

2. Identify the Values Behind Your Decisions
   Reflect on what guided you in that moment. Did you act based on clearly defined values, or did you realize later what mattered most? Write down any principles like integrity, empathy, or respect that influenced your decisions, either consciously or unconsciously.

3. Connect the Dots to Today
   How did this experience shape your leadership approach? Have those values become more central to how you lead now? Consider how this defining moment continues to influence your decisions, strategies, and interactions today.

4. Reimagine the Scenario with New Insights
    Imagine facing that same challenge again today. Armed
    with the knowledge and growth you've experienced
    since then, what would you do differently? How would
    your core values help you navigate this challenge more
    effectively now?

     DAVID L ZIMMERMAN, MSC, CPC

CHAPTER 2

BALANCING EMOTION AND LOGIC

*"Feelings are much like waves; we can't stop them,
but we can choose which ones to surf."*

—Jonatan Martensson

HAVE YOU EVER found yourself suddenly in a high-pressure situation where your instincts screamed one thing, but your rational mind urged another? This is exactly what happened to me on a stiflingly hot summer afternoon in Dallas, Texas, when I was working as a managing director for RBC Dain Rauscher, a wealth-management firm, back in the early 2000s. The air was so thick and heavy that day, our office air conditioning was struggling to keep us cool. As I gathered with my team in the conference room to discuss the quarter's targets, harsh sunlight streamed in through the floor-to-ceiling windows, creating reflections on the polished table. This accentuated the serious, dewy faces gathered around me; most of those present were sipping water to keep themselves cool and alert.

I was standing at the head of the conference table, halfway through my presentation, when the door swung open. Mark, our compliance officer, rushed in, his face drained of color, his eyes wide with urgency.

"We have a serious compliance problem, David," he blurted out, his voice strained and slightly breathless. His words landed heavily. Like bombs dropped, they created a shockwave that rippled across the room. My pulse immediately quickened, and I could practically feel the adrenaline tighten my chest. Images of newspaper headlines splashed across the country flooded my mind: *RBC Dain Rauscher Fails Compliance Requirements!*

As a flush rose across my face and my knuckles whitened as I gripped the table, every nerve in my body screamed for immediate action. My brain was shouting, "David, fix this problem now!" But I'd been in these types of situations before and knew not to give control over to my emotions. I took a deep breath and stayed quiet, even though everyone was staring at me, waiting for direction. Swallowing hard, I raised my hand, and calmly said, "Let's reconvene in an hour." My words came out steadier than I felt. The team shuffled out, glancing anxiously at each other as they departed, and I was left alone listening to the AC unit struggle. I closed my eyes, trying to steady my racing heart. Moving toward the window, I gazed down at the bustling streets below and intentionally worked to slow my breathing into a calmer rhythm. This, I knew, would gently coax my rational mind back into control. As clarity gradually returned, I started to consider ways to mitigate the risk of the situation without overreacting. Did we have all the necessary information or was more context needed? Was there an opportunity here, a chance to improve rather than merely react? What could be salvaged? It was in this deliberate effort to engage both emotional and logical thinking that I found a solution—a collaborative approach that was a path to fix our compliance issues. It was a strategy built on collaboration, transparency, and proactive change; a solution my emotional instincts alone would never have allowed me to see. When everyone returned to meet an hour later, I felt grounded and resolute. As the faces of my team, hopeful yet anxious, met mine, I felt renewed confidence to lead them through this tough period. And as I began to speak, I knew we were embarking not on damage control, but on a path of genuine improvement and resilience.

Moments like these highlight a truth many leaders overlook: decision-making isn't about suppressing emotions or relying solely on logic. Rather, it requires you to manage the interplay between the two. Neuroscience offers a powerful lens for understanding the balanced interaction required between these two key players to make effective decision-making. The amygdala, our emotional alarm system, and the frontal cortex, the center of reason and planning, both play an important role. Driven by evolutionary instinct, the amygdala reacts instantly to emotional stimuli and perceived threats. It's the part of your brain that sparks you to act quickly in a crisis. In a dangerous situation, this can be crucial. But it can also hijack your responses, leading to impulsive decisions that bypass critical thinking. Enter the frontal cortex, which looks at everything rationally and helps you weigh the pros and cons of a situation against long-term goals. This region tempers the urgency of the amygdala, weighing options, analyzing risks, and focusing on long-term goals. Understanding this dynamic can help leaders strike the right balance between instinct and analysis, especially when the stakes are high.[8] The best leaders don't just ride the waves of emotion—they learn how to surf them with precision and purpose.

EFFECTIVE LEADERS BALANCE INSTINCT AND LOGIC

We've all let our emotions get the best of us at one point or another. That's the amygdala at work. This is not a bad thing, per se. As I mentioned, this reaction is designed to respond quickly and reflexively to keep us safe in a crisis. In leadership, however, an overactive amygdala can cause impulsive decision-making that you might regret later. Neuroscientists call this an "amygdala hijack."[9] Luckily, you can train your brain to manage the amygdala. Emotional regulation (which was covered in Chapter 1) is the answer. This involves recognizing your emotional triggers and deliberately engaging your frontal cortex to balance out your amygdala. Once engaged, the frontal cortex allows you to pause, assess, and make a more intentional, less reactive, decision. Leaders who learn emotional regulation are often calmer under pressure and inspire trust within their teams.[10,11]

Imagine a high-stakes negotiation. If the amygdala is in charge, you will react reflexively rather than intentionally in that

---

[8] Davidson, R. J., & Begley, S. (2012). *The emotional life of your brain: How its unique patterns affect the way you think, feel, and live—and how you can change them.* Hudson Street Press.

[9] Goleman, D. (2006). *Emotional intelligence: Why it can matter more than IQ.* Bantam Books.

[10] Davidson, R. J., & Begley, S. (2012). The emotional life of your brain: How its unique patterns affect the way you think, feel, and live—and how you can change them. Hudson Street Press.

[11] Gross, J. J. (2015). Emotion regulation: Current status and future prospects. Psychological Inquiry, 26(1), 1–26. https://doi.org/10.1080/1047840X.2014.940781

situation. Fear, anger, and frustration will run wild, and you might agree to terms you'll regret or shut down an important relationship. But if you pause to call upon your frontal cortex, it will help you recognize those emotional triggers, step back, and recenter yourself, which will enable you to negotiate more logically and strategically. In this calmer state, you'll make a much better decision.

Professor James J. Gross, a leading researcher at Standorf University in the area of emotional regulation, highlights techniques and strategies like reappraisal to calm the amygdala in the moment and help us think about situations in a less emotional light.[12] Pair this with ongoing mindfulness work, and you're putting in place a practical system to stay composed, even in the most chaotic circumstances.

As behavior researchers Richard J. Davidson and Sharon Begley note in their book, *The Emotional Life of Your Brain*, effective leaders regulate emotional responses in the amygdala while engaging the frontal cortex for strategic planning.[13] I call this the Emotion-Logic Nexus. In high-stakes situations, emotional regulation needs to meet strategic thinking in order to produce decisions that are not only effective but also empathetic and inclusive. Leaders who operate in this nexus navigate complexity without losing sight of the human factor. They excel at making decisions that resonate on both a logical and emotional level. This fosters respect, trust, and team cohesion.

---

[12] Gross, J. J. (2015). Emotion regulation: Current status and future prospects. Psychological Inquiry, 26(1), 1–26. https://doi.org/10.1080/1047840X.2014.940781

[13] Davidson, R. J., & Begley, S. (2012). The emotional life of your brain: How its unique patterns affect the way you think, feel, and live—and how you can change them. Hudson Street Press.

KEY TAKEAWAYS

Moments of crisis often expose a leader's default settings, but they also offer the greatest opportunity for growth. We've explored how the amygdala's lightning fast alarm system and the frontal cortex's deliberate reasoning must operate in concert if you want to make leadership decisions that protect both today's reputation and tomorrow's strategy. The formula is deceptively simple: You need to pause and regulate before you engage and communicate. Buy yourself some time. Settle yourself down. A single deep breath or a brief adjournment is often enough to interrupt an emotional cascade. Name the emotion you are feeling. The act of labeling dampens the amygdala's activity and reroutes processing to the frontal cortex. Once you feel calm and back in control, invite logic and diverse viewpoints to the table. Ask your team, "What data are we missing?" "Who else should we ask to weigh in on this decision?" This is how you and your team get to see the whole picture and make truly informed and sound decisions. Practiced consistently, this cycle rewires neural pathways, creating leaders who remain composed under pressure and inspire confidence in turbulent times.

By training your brain to surf the waves of emotion rather than be swallowed by them, you model maturity, safeguard strategic thinking, and signal to your organization that *urgent* does not have to mean *reckless*. As you move forward, the practice of auditing recent highstakes choices will help you maintain the right approach. Where did emotion override analysis? Where did overanalysis stall momentum? These practices are the hallmark of a leader who is capable of balancing heart and head for lasting impact and high performance.

Emotional regulation is critical for maintaining clarity and stability in leadership decisions.

     DAVID L ZIMMERMAN, MSC, CPC

The Emotion-Logic Nexus enables leaders to balance empathy and strategy effectively.

Leaders who integrate emotional and logical thinking create more inclusive and impactful outcomes.

CASE STUDY: ANGELA MERKEL NAVIGATES A MIGRATION CRISIS

Let's rewind to a pivotal moment for Europe in 2015. Countries across the continent were grappling with a surge of refugees and migrants fleeing war, instability, and economic hardship.[14] The numbers were unprecedented, with more than a million people seeking safety and opportunity. Many of these people arrived in Germany.[15] It was a moment that tested the resolve of governments, and it was here that Angela Merkel, then Chancellor of Germany, made a decision that would forever define her leadership: she opened Germany's borders.[16]

Her approach was bold and grounded in empathy. While others hesitated, she declared, "We can do this," framing the refugee crisis as an opportunity for solidarity and humanitarian action.[17] Her decision reflected Germany's post-World War II values of openness and justice. Merkel recognized the complexity of the situation but believed in Germany's capacity to respond with both compassion and pragmatism.

---

[14] The Guardian. (2015). Refugee crisis: How the image of a drowned child changed history. Retrieved from *https://www.theguardian.com*

[15] Pew Research Center. (2016). Europe's asylum seeker surge. Retrieved from *https://www.pewresearch.org*

[16] The New York Times. (2015). Merkel's choice. Retrieved from *https://www.nytimes.com*

[17] Der Spiegel. (2015). Merkel: "We can do it." Retrieved from *https://www.spiegel.de*

Critics of Merkel's decision argued that the rapid influx of refugees posed logistical and political challenges, but her leadership left a lasting impact. Periodicals like *The Economist* described Merkel's actions as "moral courage" in the face of widespread uncertainty.[18] By combining empathy with strategic action, she set an example of how leaders can respond to complex crises without losing sight of their principles.

What set Merkel's leadership apart was her ability to balance emotional intelligence with a clear strategy. She acknowledged German citizens' concerns about the strain on resources and the challenges of integrating such a large number of people, while steadfastly emphasizing the need for compassion. By presenting a clear vision of inclusion—without dismissing the challenges it might bring—Merkel balanced empathy with transparency to build trust with her people in a moment of great uncertainty. She worked tirelessly to create pathways for integration, from language programs to employment initiatives. These measures reflected her belief that, with the right support, Germany could not only welcome refugees but benefit from their contributions in the long run.[19] She understood the broader implications of the crisis and sought collaborative solutions. One of her key moves was negotiating the EU-Turkey deal in 2016, which helped manage migration flows while supporting humanitarian efforts in Turkey.[20] This initiative highlighted Merkel's ability to address immediate needs while working toward systemic, long-term solutions.

---

[18]   The Economist. (2015). Merkel's moral courage. Retrieved from *https://www.economist.com*

[19]   Der Spiegel. (2015). Merkel: "We can do it." Retrieved from *https://www.spiegel.de*

[20]   Reuters. (2016). EU-Turkey refugee deal explained. Retrieved from *https://www.reuters.com*

From a neuroscience perspective, Merkel's leadership illustrates the balance between emotional response of the amygdala and the rational, strategic response of the prefrontal cortex. Merkel's calm demeanor and deliberate actions showcased this balance, enabling her to lead with both compassion and foresight. Merkel also reframed the refugee crisis as an opportunity for growth. She emphasized that integrating refugees could help address Germany's demographic challenges, including an aging workforce and labor shortages. "If we manage to integrate these refugees," she said, "we can strengthen our economy and our society."[21] This forward-looking perspective aligns with Gross's research on cognitive reappraisal, which highlights the power of reframing challenges to promote adaptive thinking.[22] By prioritizing the human impact of her decisions without losing sight of strategic objectives, Merkel exemplified how to operate within the Emotion-Logic Nexus.

REFLECTION

Ask yourself the following questions and write your answers in your journal. After, take time to reflect on your discoveries.

1. What is a recent decision that you made under pressure?

2. Which emotional-regulation techniques did you use?

3. Is empathy part of your leadership style?

4. Which leaders do you admire most and why?

---

21 Der Spiegel. (2015). Merkel: "We can do it." Retrieved from *https://www.spiegel.de*

22 Gross, J. J. (2015). Emotion regulation: Current status and future prospects. *Psychological Inquiry*, 26(1), 1–26. https://doi.org/10.1080/1047840X.2014.940781

5. How do you balance your emotions and logical thinking as a leader?

SELF-AUDIT

Rate yourself on a scale from one to ten, where one means "rarely or not at all" and ten means "frequently or very well."

1. I recognize when emotions influence my decisions.

   1 2 3 4 5 6 7 8 9 10

2. I take deliberate steps to regulate emotional impulses.

   1 2 3 4 5 6 7 8 9 10

3. I actively engage logical reasoning for long-term impact assessment.

   1 2 3 4 5 6 7 8 9 10

4. I consider the emotional implications of my decisions for others.

   1 2 3 4 5 6 7 8 9 10

5. I use empathy to build trust and rapport within my team.

   1 2 3 4 5 6 7 8 9 10

6. I rely on both emotion and logic to guide my leadership approach.

   1 2 3 4 5 6 7 8 9 10

7. I maintain composure in emotionally charged situations.

   1 2 3 4 5 6 7 8 9 10

8. I prioritize emotional intelligence as a leadership skill.

   1 2 3 4 5 6 7 8 9 10

9. I encourage team members to balance empathy with rationale.

1   2   3   4   5   6   7   8   9   10

10. I consistently integrate emotional and logical considerations in decision-making.

1   2   3   4   5   6   7   8   9   10

EXERCISE: DEVELOP AN EMOTION-LOGIC CHECKLIST

In a journal, outline a recent decision where both emotion and logic were involved. Describe how each factor influenced your decision-making process and identify areas where you could strengthen this balance in future situations. Consider what emotional responses emerged and how logical analysis could have enhanced the outcome. This exercise aims to refine the integration of empathy and rationality, creating a more balanced leadership style.

CHAPTER 3

STRESS, SLEEP, AND HIGH STAKES

*"Almost everything will work again if you unplug it
for a few minutes, including you."*

—Anne Lamott

ARRIVED AT THE office at 4:00 a.m. on a rainy Thursday morning in September. The city lights beyond my office window at PaineWebber glimmered faintly as I studied the cluttered landscape of my desk. It was covered in papers and scribbled notes, financial projections, and critical evaluations of an important recruitment deal. My tie hung loosely around my neck, shirt sleeves rolled up, as I stared at the screen full of spreadsheets, my eyes dry and burning from exhaustion. I clung to an ice-cold Diet Coke, but the sharp, fizzy bite of soda did little to dispel the fog that had settled over my exhausted brain.

The team I was recruiting—a coveted group managing assets worth over $600 million—represented an immense opportunity for our district. It was a transformative acquisition that required my sharpest judgment and most thoughtful consideration—but at the time, I was so overworked and under-rested that clarity eluded me. I'd thought I was being disciplined by putting in the extra hours, but it just so turns out that human beings are like any other machine: without regular maintenance, we'll lose our ability to function optimally and eventually fall apart.

I was about halfway into the meeting when I realized that my every attempt to analyze the situation was disintegrating into fragmented thoughts. With tense muscles and a dull headache, my body was crying out for rest amid the sustained stress and anxiety of the project. My brain and body were shouting urgently for a break, but I didn't listen. In the wee hours of the following morning, with desperation eclipsing logic, I hastily typed an email. It was brief, curt, and definitive: "We want to halt negotiations immediately." All it took was a swift tap of the "send" button to impulsively seal my fate.

As the message disappeared into cyberspace, a rush of relief momentarily swept over me. But in the days that followed, shockwaves rippled through our office and beyond. Missed goals, setbacks, and a slew of incredulous, unanswered questions had cast a pall that was so heavy, it suffocated all traces of our company morale. I was haunted by persistent reminders of what had been sacrificed to fatigue and stress. Reflecting back on this stressful time in my early career, the lesson is clear: leadership demands more than dedication and effort—it requires intentional balance and rejuvenation. Otherwise, stress and fatigue lead to poor decision-making that can sometimes be catastrophic. That early-morning moment in the silence of my office remains a vivid reminder of the critical importance of rest and clarity in the art of leadership. I made a huge mistake and vowed never to lead from such a state of imbalance again.

Every leader has been there. The long hours, the pressure to deliver, and the belief that pushing through the exhaustion is some sort of badge of honor. But the truth is, fatigue and stress are silent saboteurs that cloud judgment and sap cognitive clarity and resilience. In fact, neuroscience reveals that fatigue and stress impair our ability to lead effectively, hindering emotional regulation, stifling creativity, and leading to reactive, rather than intentional, decision-making.[23,24] Remember, leadership isn't just about making decisions—it's about making the *right* decisions. That requires your mind, body, and spirit to be in top form.

When was the last time you made a high-stakes decision after a sleepless night or during a particularly stressful period? Did you notice how it impacted your ability to focus or evaluate your options clearly? As mentioned earlier in this book, leadership demands cognitive clarity, adaptability, and resilience. Yet many leaders underestimate how chronic stress and inadequate sleep undermine those core disciplines. Sleep does more than restore energy—it consolidates memories, helps process emotions, and primes the brain for creativity and critical thinking. Chronic stress and lack of sleep disrupt these processes, fostering emotional exhaustion, mental fatigue, and poor judgment.

EUSTRESS VERSUS DISTRESS

There is more than one type of stress. Eustress is the type of stress that motivates you to perform at your best. Think of the

23   Walker, M. P. (2017). *Why we sleep: Unlocking the power of sleep and dreams.* Scribner.

24   Dinges, D. F., & Basner, M. (2018). The impact of sleep deprivation on cognitive performance and decision-making. *Annual Review of Psychology, 69,* 275–299. *https://doi.org/10.1146/annurev-psych-122216-011613*

focus you gain before delivering an important presentation or the energy that drives you to meet a tight deadline. This form of stress activates your body's natural "fight or flight" response in a controlled and beneficial way, enhancing performance when managed appropriately.[25] It's mostly a *positive* type of stress. In leadership, eustress leads to:

ENHANCED PRODUCTIVITY

Moderate stress can improve concentration and problem-solving, keeping you sharp.

- **Cognitive Growth**
  Challenging situations can push you beyond your comfort zone, helping you develop new skills and fostering resilience.

- **Stronger Confidence**
  Successfully navigating eustress reinforces your ability to face future challenges with poise.

The opposite of eustress is *distress*, which is when stress becomes chronic, excessive, or unmanageable. While eustress inspires action, distress overwhelms the mind and body, leading to exhaustion, impaired judgment, and diminished emotional control. For leaders, this can erode decision-making capabilities and strain relationships. The key characteristics of distress include:

- **Cognitive Overload**
  This is when you have difficulty concentrating, memory lapses, and experience indecisiveness.

---

[25]   Selye, H. (1974). *Stress without distress*. J.B. Lippincott Company.

- **Physical Symptoms**
  Chronic fatigue, tension headaches, and disrupted sleep patterns are all symptoms of distress.

- **Emotional Instability**
  When people are in distress, they experience heightened anxiety, irritability, or feelings of being overwhelmed.

Research shows that chronic distress floods the brain with cortisol, a stress hormone that impairs the prefrontal cortex, which governs logical reasoning and decision-making. Conversely, cortisol overstimulates the amygdala. This imbalance can lead to impulsive actions and difficulty navigating complex problems.[26,27]

HOW DO YOU STRIKE THE RIGHT BALANCE?

The goal isn't to eliminate stress entirely. That's impossible—and trying to do something that's impossible, well, might stress you out! The goal is to learn how to manage stress effectively. Leaders who harness eustress while mitigating distress create an optimal environment for high performance and well-being. Achieving this balance requires:

- Self-Awareness
  Identify your personal stress thresholds and triggers. Which situations energize you, and which drain you?

---

[26] Sapolsky, R. M. (2004). *Why zebras don't get ulcers: The acclaimed guide to stress, stress-related diseases, and coping* (3rd ed.). Holt Paperbacks.

[27] McEwen, B. S., & Stellar, E. (1993). Stress and the individual: Mechanisms leading to disease. *Archives of Internal Medicine, 153*(18), 2093–2101. *https://doi.org/10.1001/archinte.1993.0041 0180039004*

- **Strategic Recovery**
  Incorporate practices like mindfulness, exercise, and regular breaks to reduce the long-term effects of distress.

- **Reframing Challenges**
  View stressful situations as opportunities for growth and learning rather than obstacles, shifting from a mindset of fear to one of curiosity and resilience.[28]

To harness good stress while avoiding the pitfalls of distress:

- Break challenges into manageable steps, maintaining focus and control.

- Prioritize tasks to prevent stress from becoming unmanageable.

- Celebrate progress and small victories to sustain motivation and positivity.

By understanding and differentiating between eustress and distress, leaders can navigate challenges with greater clarity and intention, using stress as a tool for growth rather than a source of harm.

WHAT DOES SUSTAINABLE LEADERSHIP LOOK LIKE?

I'll answer with three simple concepts that build on the ideas we've just explored: effective stress-management, sufficient sleep, and self-care. This seems like a manageable to-do list for sustainable leadership, right? Apparently not. As a nation, we're headed in the wrong direction. In 2024, the American Psychological Association's annual *Stress in America* report revealed that "43% of American adults reported feeling more

---

[28] Dweck, C. S. (2006). *Mindset: The new psychology of success.* Random House.

anxious than the previous year, with many attributing this anxiety to increased stress." That's up a whopping eleven percentage points in two years. News on the sleep front is equally disturbing. According to a 2024 Gallup Poll:

> For the first time in Gallup polling since 2001, a majority of U.S. adults, 57%, say they would feel better if they got more sleep, while 42% say they get as much sleep as they need. This is nearly a reversal of the figures last measured in 2013, when 56% of Americans got the sleep they needed and 43% did not. Americans' perception that they aren't getting enough sleep is borne out by the diminished number of hours of sleep they report getting per night.
>
> These differences in average sleep reflect substantial changes over time in the percentage of U.S. adults sleeping eight or more versus five hours or less per night. In 1942, 59% were getting eight-plus hours of sleep, while only 3% reported getting five hours or less. By 1990, the percentage reporting eight or more hours had fallen to 27%, while the proportion getting five or less was up to 14%. Today, a quarter are still getting eight-plus hours, but the percentage getting five or less has risen to 20%.

These worrisome trends are also showing up in corporate America. In fact, corporate America's stats are worse than the general population's. Global leadership firm DDI interviewed 11,000 leaders for their *Global Leadership Forecast 2025*, and the revelations are disturbing. More than half (54%) of leaders expressed serious concerns about burnout and 40% stated that they have contemplated leaving their leadership position specifically to protect their well-being. Finally, a striking 71%

of leaders reported increased levels of stress. It seems that there might be a leadership sustainability crisis at hand!

Though some corporate cultures continue to glorify leaders who power through long hours, high stress, and sleepless nights, this approach is clearly unsustainable. Research shows that chronic stress and sleep deprivation damage the prefrontal cortex, the brain region responsible for logical reasoning and decision-making. Without adequate rest, even the most experienced leaders struggle with focus, creativity, and emotional stability.[29,30]

Sustainable leadership requires leaders to actively manage stress and prioritize sleep, so they are better equipped to handle the complexities of leadership. The phase of sleep characterized by Rapid Eye Movement (REM), when most dreams occur, is especially important as it facilitates emotional regulation, memory consolidation, emotional processing, and overall brain health.[31] This stage of the sleep cycle is essential for leaders who need to maintain clarity to deal with the high-stakes scenarios their jobs demand.

For leadership to be sustainable, leaders must cultivate stamina, resilience, and other habits that mitigate stress's long-term negative effects. Clearly, based on current data, these habits haven't been adopted at the required level. Otherwise, we wouldn't be seeing the rising stress levels that we're seeing in 2025. Being a healthy, well-rested, focused, and calm leader

---

[29]   Walker, M. P. (2017). *Why we sleep: Unlocking the power of sleep and dreams*. Scribner.

[30]   Sapolsky, R. M. (2004). *Why zebras don't get ulcers: The acclaimed guide to stress, stress-related diseases, and coping* (3rd ed.). Holt Paperbacks.

[31]   Stickgold, R. (2005). Sleep-dependent memory consolidation. *Nature, 437*(7063), 1272–1278. *https://doi.org/10.1038/nature04286*

is not a luxury these days—it's a necessity. By prioritizing rest, relaxation, and other disciplines that sustain mental health and balance, leaders can continue to be high-performers for the long term, making sound decisions even under continued pressure.

THE REST-RESILIENCE CYCLE

I've coined a phrase called the Rest-Resilience Cycle to offer a new perspective on how rest and resilience are interconnected. Rather than viewing rest as a passive activity, this model positions it as an active strategy for building and maintaining resilience. Leaders who integrate intentional rest into their routines are better equipped to handle stress, adapt to challenges, and sustain high performance. The three phases of the Rest-Resilience Cycle are:

1. Rest Fuels Renewal. Quality sleep and intentional rest periods allow the brain to recover from cognitive fatigue, restoring emotional balance and sharpening focus.[32]

2. Resilience Enhances Response. With restored mental clarity, leaders are better prepared to respond to stressors constructively. This adaptability creates a feedback loop where resilience supports rest, and rest builds resilience.

3. Active Recovery Completes the Cycle. Practices like mindfulness, meditation, and structured downtime, which complete the cycle by actively reducing stress hormones and improving overall well-being.[33]

---

[32] Walker, M. P. (2017). *Why we sleep: Unlocking the power of sleep and dreams.* Scribner.

[33] Dinges, D. F., & Basner, M. (2018). The impact of sleep deprivation on cognitive performance and decision-making. *Annual Review of Psychology, 69,* 275–299. *https://doi.org/10.1146/annurev-psych-122216-011613*

Leaders who neglect this important cycle risk falling into patterns of exhaustion and diminished performance. Conversely, those who embrace it cultivate a sustainable approach to leadership, fueling achievement through continual rejuvenation. Understanding the physiological and psychological interplay between stress and sleep reveals how these factors shape leadership performance. Here are three critical insights:

1. **Cortisol Causes Decision Fatigue**
   As I've mentioned, stress triggers the release of cortisol, a hormone that helps manage short-term challenges. However, prolonged exposure to cortisol impairs the prefrontal cortex, reducing cognitive flexibility and increasing impulsivity.[34] Decision fatigue sets in as mental stamina depletes, making it harder for leaders to evaluate complex information critically.

2. **Emotional Regulation Requires REM**
   The REM phase of sleep plays a vital role in processing emotions and maintaining balance. Without it, leaders may experience heightened emotional reactivity, compromising their ability to remain composed under pressure.[35] This stage of sleep is crucial for managing stress responses and ensuring rational decision-making.

SLEEP PROVIDES A COGNITIVE REBOOT

During deep sleep, the brain consolidates memories, organizes information, and prepares for new learning. This "cognitive reboot" is essential for leaders who must process and act on

---

[34] Sapolsky, R. M. (2004). *Why zebras don't get ulcers: The acclaimed guide to stress, stress-related diseases, and coping* (3rd ed.). Holt Paperbacks.

[35] Walker, M. P. (2017). *Why we sleep: Unlocking the power of sleep and dreams*. Scribner.

complex data quickly and accurately. Chronic sleep deprivation disrupts this process, hindering strategic thinking and innovation.[36]

KEY TAKEAWAYS

The earlymorning misstep that cost my district a $600 million opportunity is more than a cautionary tale, it is a mirror reflecting a truth that too many leaders ignore: your judgment is only as sharp as your rest is deep. Throughout this chapter we explored the neuroscience behind fatigue, the fine line between eustress and distress, and the Rest Resilience Cycle that converts disciplined recovery into sustained performance. The evidence is unambiguous: chronic sleep debt and unrelenting stress are not signs of dedication—they are corrosive forces that shrink the prefrontal cortex, inflame the amygdala, and turn decisive executives into reactive bystanders. The antidote is within reach. By treating sleep as a strategic asset, scheduling recovery with the same rigor you give to revenue meetings, and reframing pressure as purposeful eustress, you create the cognitive bandwidth to lead with clarity. Build microbreaks into your calendar, protect a nonnegotiable sleep window, delegate before depletion sets in, and practice mindfulness and breath work to reset cortisol levels in real time. These are not perks, but rather cornerstones of sustainable leadership. Leadership in highstakes environments will never be stressfree. But when you anchor your performance to intentional rest and self-care, you become a better leader with the required stamina. So shut down your devices, dim the lights, and give your brain the seven to eight hours it needs to convert grit into

---

[36] Stickgold, R. (2005). Sleep-dependent memory consolidation. *Nature, 437*(7063), 1272–1278. *https://doi.org/10.1038/nature 04286*

wisdom. Your future decisions, and the people who depend on them, are counting on it.

- **Rest is an active leadership strategy.** Leaders who view rest as a proactive tool, not a passive indulgence, enhance their cognitive flexibility, emotional regulation, and overall effectiveness.

- **The Rest-Resilience Cycle creates sustainable performance.** By integrating rest and recovery into your daily routine, you can sustain resilience over time, avoiding the burnout and decision fatigue that hinder long-term success.

- **Stress and rest are interconnected.** Understanding the physiological and psychological interplay between stress and sleep enables leaders to manage both more effectively, ensuring they lead with clarity and composure during high-stakes challenges.

CASE STUDY: ARNE SORENSON'S QUIET STRENGTH AND THE POWER OF BALANCED LEADERSHIP

While many leaders push through stress and burnout as a badge of honor, Arne Sorenson, the former CEO of Marriott International, modeled a different kind of leadership—one that fused high performance with humility, intentional recovery, and deep personal resilience. His story offers a compelling counter-narrative to the glorification of overwork and reveals how grace under pressure, not just grit, defines sustainable leadership. When Sorenson was appointed CEO of Marriott in 2012, he made history as the company's first non-family CEO. Known for his calm demeanor, deep empathy, and bold strategic thinking, he was tasked with navigating the global expansion of the hospitality giant, culminating in Marriott's $13 billion acquisition of Starwood Hotels in 2016, a move that catapulted the company to the top of the global hotel industry.[37]

However, leadership clarity doesn't come from intensity alone. In 2019, Sorenson publicly announced he had been diagnosed with pancreatic cancer. Rather than withdrawing from the spotlight or pretending nothing had changed, he openly acknowledged the reality of his condition and made intentional adjustments. He scheduled time away for treatment, publicly delegated certain operational responsibilities, and, most notably, began modeling what responsible, sustainable leadership could look like under enormous personal and professional pressure.[38]

During the COVID-19 pandemic, when the travel industry was decimated, Sorenson delivered a message to his employees that stunned the business world. Frail from chemotherapy, with visible signs of his treatment, he addressed more than 174,000 Marriott associates around the world in a heartfelt video. He didn't mask his vulnerability. Instead, he leaned into it. His message: We are suffering, but we will persevere. And we will do so with humanity and dignity.[39]

What Sorenson demonstrated wasn't just executive responsibility; it was leadership stamina rooted in intentional choices

---

[37] Dweck, C. S. (2006). *Mindset: The new psychology of success.* Random House.

[38] Dinges, D. F., & Basner, M. (2018). The impact of sleep deprivation on cognitive performance and decision-making. *Annual Review of Psychology, 69,* 275–299. *https://doi.org/10.1146/annurev-psych-122216-011613*

[39] Hargrave, M. (2018). Elon Musk says Model 3 production woes have made life "excruciating." *Investopedia.* Retrieved from *https://www.investopedia.com*

about energy, rest, and prioritization. Even while battling a terminal illness, he resisted the urge to operate from burnout or bravado. He made space for rest, trusted his team, and gave himself permission to slow down without giving up. His poise and clarity were not the result of relentless output, but rather the product of deep internal alignment, strategic delegation, and emotional regulation—qualities neuroscience confirms are supported by adequate sleep and stress recovery.[40]

Arne Sorenson's story teaches us that sustainable leadership isn't about defying our limits, it's about respecting them. His quiet strength, balanced approach, and intentional recovery practices offer a vital blueprint for any leader facing high-stakes decisions and unrelenting pressure. Leaders who prioritize self-care and trust their teams not only preserve their own health and clarity but also create conditions for long-term organizational resilience.

REFLECTION

Ask yourself the following questions and write your answers in your journal. After, take time to reflect on your discoveries.

1. How does stress currently influence your decision-making?

2. What steps can you take to improve your relationship with sleep and rest?

3. How can you model a culture of resilience within your organization?

---

[40] McEwen, B. S., & Stellar, E. (1993). Stress and the individual: Mechanisms leading to disease. *Archives of Internal Medicine, 153*(18), 2093–2101. *https://doi.org/10.1001/archinte.1993.00410180039004*

4. What lessons can you draw from Arne Sorenson's journey to balance ambition with recovery?

5. How can you incorporate rest into your leadership strategy to sustain long-term performance?

SELF-AUDIT

Rate yourself on a scale from one to ten, where one means "rarely or not at all" and ten means "frequently or very well."

1. I prioritize sleep as part of my leadership performance.

   1   2   3   4   5   6   7   8   9   10

2. I proactively manage stress to maintain clarity.

   1   2   3   4   5   6   7   8   9   10

3. I establish clear boundaries to protect rest and recovery time.

   1   2   3   4   5   6   7   8   9   10

4. I model sustainable work habits for my team.

   1   2   3   4   5   6   7   8   9   10

5. I practice mindfulness or other techniques to manage stress.

   1   2   3   4   5   6   7   8   9   10

6. I recognize the signs of decision fatigue and take steps to address it.

   1   2   3   4   5   6   7   8   9   10

7. I incorporate breaks and downtime into my daily routine.

   1   2   3   4   5   6   7   8   9   10

8. I approach stress as an opportunity for growth rather than a barrier.

    DAVID L ZIMMERMAN, MSC, CPC

| 1 | 2 | 3 | 4 | 5 | 6 | 7 | 8 | 9 | 10 |

9. I encourage my team to prioritize resilience alongside productivity.

| 1 | 2 | 3 | 4 | 5 | 6 | 7 | 8 | 9 | 10 |

10. I understand the role of sleep in maintaining cognitive flexibility and emotional regulation.

| 1 | 2 | 3 | 4 | 5 | 6 | 7 | 8 | 9 | 10 |

EXERCISE: CREATE A REST AND RESILIENCE PLAN

This exercise will help you craft a personalized strategy for managing stress and prioritizing rest, enabling you to sustain high performance and resilience.

1. **Identify Stressors**
   Reflect on the key stressors in your leadership role. Are they tied to tight deadlines, interpersonal conflicts, or decision-making pressure? Write down the most common triggers and assess how they impact your mental and emotional state.

2. **Assess Your Current Rest Practices**
   How much sleep do you typically get? What is the quality of that sleep? Consider your habits around breaks and downtime. Are they structured and intentional, or sporadic and reactive?

3. **Set Boundaries**
   Establish clear limits for work hours, screen time, and engagement with stressful tasks. For example, set a rule to stop checking emails an hour before bedtime.

4. **Create a Daily Rest Routine**
    Design a routine that incorporates restorative practices like mindfulness, meditation, or physical activity. Include time for reflection and relaxation.

5. **Develop a Contingency Plan for High-Stress Periods**
    Outline how you will manage rest during demanding times. For instance, schedule power naps, delegate tasks, or commit to shorter but higher-quality rest periods.

6. **Monitor and Adjust**
    Track your progress weekly. How well are you adhering to your plan? What results are you noticing in your mood, energy, and decision-making clarity? Refine your approach as needed.

CHAPTER 4

MOTIVATION AND HIGH PERFORMANCE

*"Effort and courage are not enough without
purpose and direction."*

—John F. Kennedy

I REMEMBER MY DOOR opened quietly one Tuesday when I was the vice president and district manager for PaineWebber in Nashville, Tennessee. The top-performing senior financial advisor in the region stepped into my office for his quarterly review. As his boss, I was all smiles, because his numbers were great, as always. But I noticed that his shoulders were slumped, betraying his usual confidence. He eased himself into the chair across from me with a deep sigh and didn't make eye contact—again, odd. Instead, he just stared at the steam rising from the cup of coffee in front of him. We exchanged brief pleasantries before diving into our usual quarterly discussion. As I began outlining potential strategies for team restructuring and upcoming objectives, I noticed his gaze drifting away. He wasn't listening to a word I was saying—again, this was very uncharacteristic.

I paused. "Kevin, is everything okay?"

He drew in a long, slow breath before answering. "Listen, David," he began, his voice heavy with emotion. "I know I'm good at what I do—really good. But I feel like I'm running on empty. I keep hitting every target, but I don't feel any connection to my work anymore. It's just numbers."

His confession resonated deeply with me. I could sense the depth of his struggle. The external accolades and bonuses no longer gave him a sense of fulfillment. Looking across the table at Kevin's fatigued expression, I felt a mix of concern and responsibility settle heavily on my shoulders. He was our best financial advisor—reliable, driven, respected—and yet, he was unraveling quietly under the weight of invisible pressure. Not because he was weak, but because he was human.

I put the agenda aside, leaned in, and said, "Let's not talk numbers today. Let's talk about you."

This moment marked a shift, not just in our conversation, but in my understanding of what leadership truly required. I didn't need to motivate Kevin with more goals or accolades; I needed to help him reconnect to his *why*. We spent the rest of the meeting discussing what had once brought him joy in the work, what he felt was missing, and what he needed to recalibrate—not just his performance, but his sense of purpose. His issues didn't get solved in a single conversation, but a door had been opened for both of us. For the first time in a long while, I saw that sustaining high performance was about more than pushing people to achieve—it was about helping them align achievement with meaning. That insight changed how I led from that day forward. I began paying closer attention to the warning signs behind high-functioning burnout. I checked in more deeply, not just more often. Kevin did eventually find his rhythm again—not by doing more, but by doing things differently. And so, did I.

The conversation was a stark reminder that success without purpose is hollow. I reflected on my own leadership journey. What was driving me? Was it the prestige of the role, the financial rewards, or something deeper? I thought back to the moments that truly energized me: mentoring younger advisors, recruiting new financial advisors, and building teams to drive the business and support a bigger vision of client success. That was my fuel, my motivational driver.

As leaders, we often focus on external goals, hitting numbers, achieving milestones, or fulfilling organizational objectives. But true motivation is not external—it's internal, rooted in what gives us meaning and energy. Without understanding our core motivational drivers, we risk burnout, disconnection, or leading with a lack of authenticity, which is something others can sense. Motivation isn't just about ambition, it's the energy that powers our purpose, engagement, and commitment. When motivational drivers are aligned with leadership vision, it becomes a force multiplier that energizing leadership, inspires teams, and enriches entire organizations. Peeling back the layers to lead with alignment can amplify your impact, energize you, and help you build a foundation for lasting success.

WHAT MOTIVATES YOU AND YOUR TEAM?

Yes, understanding what drives you and your people can be a game-changer. By tapping into motivational theories, leaders gain deeper insights. Here's a closer look at some key motivation theories and how they apply to leadership:

Maslow's Hierarchy of Needs

Abraham Maslow introduced a framework that suggests people are motivated by a series of needs, starting with the basics like food and safety and moving all the way up to self-actualization.[41] For leaders, this model can be a helpful lens to assess where they're currently operating. Are you focused on foundational needs, or have you moved toward higher-order aspirations like purpose and contribution? Recognizing this can help you align your decisions with what truly matters to you at this stage in your journey.

Self-Determination Theory (SDT)

Deci and Ryan's Self-Determination Theory highlights three core psychological needs: autonomy, competence, and relatedness.[42] Motivation thrives when these needs are met. For leaders, this means creating an environment where people feel empowered to make decisions, develop their skills, and build meaningful connections. When these elements are present, not only do you feel more engaged, but your team does too. It's a win-win for building an energized and motivated workplace.

Intrinsic vs. Extrinsic Motivation

Ryan and Deci differentiate between **intrinsic motivation**, doing something because you find it

---

[41] Maslow, A. H. (1943). A theory of human motivation. *Psychological Review, 50*(4), 370–396. https://doi.org/10.1037/h0054346

[42] Deci, E. L., & Ryan, R. M. (1985). *Intrinsic motivation and self-determination in human behavior*. Springer.

inherently satisfying, and **extrinsic motivation**, which is driven by external rewards like money or recognition.[43] For leaders, leaning into intrinsic motivators can make all the difference. When you're focused on work that brings you genuine fulfillment, you're not just more engaged, you're more likely to stick with it over the long haul. It's about finding meaning, not just meeting expectations.

Purpose-Driven Leadership

Purpose-driven leaders, as described by Nick Craig and Scott Snook, bring a unique strength to their roles.[44] They view challenges as opportunities for growth and adapt more easily to change. When your motivation is anchored in purpose, it creates a guiding force for your decisions. It's not just about getting through the day—it's about aligning your choices with your values and leaving a lasting impact.

By understanding the basics of these motivational theories, leaders can reflect on what truly drives them and use that insight to make more intentional, purpose-driven decisions. But this isn't about theory; it's about applying the concepts in these theories to foster personal and professional growth for you and your team.

---

[43] Deci, E. L., & Ryan, R. M. (2000). The "what" and "why" of goal pursuits: Human needs and the self-determination of behavior. *Psychological Inquiry, 11*(4), 227–268. https://doi.org/10.1207/S15327965PLI1104_01

[44] Craig, N., & Snook, S. (2014). From purpose to impact. *Harvard Business Review, 92*(5), 104–111.

LEARN TO ALIGN DRIVERS AND INCENTIVES

Leadership grounded in purpose-driven motivation is both powerful and enduring. Decades of research, including work by psychologists Edward Deci and Richard Ryan at Rochester University, underscore the importance of intrinsic motivation (the motivation that stems from our personal values and passions).[45] For leaders, intrinsic motivation can drive sustained effort and commitment, genuine satisfaction, and deeper engagement. They can lead with authentic conviction, drive, and purpose. Conversely, those who rely primarily on external or extrinsic motivators, such as financial rewards or public recognition, achieve short-term gains but often struggle to maintain adaptability and engagement over time.[46]

The challenge and opportunity for leaders lies in identifying and cultivating intrinsic motivations that resonate with individual aspirations and the organization's collective mission.

This is called **incentive alignment**. It begins with an understanding of your intrinsic motivators and your team's. What fuels you and your team's energy and focus? It could be mastering new skills, having the autonomy to lead important projects, or finding purpose in the impact of your work.[47] Once you can identify these key motivators, it's time to align them with your organization's broader goals. When an authentic alignment is achieved, it boosts motivation, builds resilience, and strengthens commitment. Research in organizational psychology reinforces the benefit of aligning personal values

---

[45] Baumeister, R. F., & Vohs, K. D. (2016). *Handbook of self-regulation: Research, theory, and applications* (3rd ed.). Guilford Press.

[46] Baumeister, R. F., & Vohs, K. D. (2016). *Handbook of self-regulation: Research, theory, and applications* (3rd ed.). Guilford Press.

[47] Pink, D. H. (2011). *Drive: The surprising truth about what motivates us.* Riverhead Books.

with professional roles. Organizational Psychologist Amy Wrzesniewhki and her team found that individuals who align their work with their personal values tend to perform at higher levels and show more creativity.[48] For leaders, bringing these values into their roles doesn't just benefit them, it elevates everyone else in the entire organization.

Leaders who reach alignment often find themselves operating in a "flow state," where their work feels natural, fulfilling, and energizing. Why? Because purpose-driven leadership is about tapping into human desire to contribute in meaningful ways. As Author Daniel Pink suggests in his book, *Drive: The Surprising Truth About What Motivates Us*, when leaders are motivated by purpose, they unlock a wellspring of energy that empowers both themselves and their teams.[49]

Imagine a leader passionate about social impact aligning their values with the company's corporate social responsibility (CSR) initiatives. This alignment gives their work greater meaning while also advancing the organization's mission. Professor Archie Carroll of the University of Georgia and Professor Kareem Shabana of Central Connecticut State University found that when employee motivations align with CSR efforts, it strengthens organizational commitment and improves relationships with external stakeholders.[50] Similarly, Deci and

---

[48] Wrzesniewski, A., McCauley, C., Rozin, P., & Schwartz, B. (1997). Jobs, careers, and callings: People's relations to their work. *Journal of Research in Personality, 31*(1), 21–33. https://doi.org/10.1006/jrpe.1997.2162

[49] Pink, D. H. (2011). *Drive: The surprising truth about what motivates us.* Riverhead Books.

[50] Carroll, A. B., & Shabana, K. M. (2010). The business case for corporate social responsibility: A review of concepts, research, and practice. *International Journal of Management Reviews, 12*(1), 85–105. https://doi.org/10.1111/j.1468-2370.2009.00275.x

Ryan observed that syncing intrinsic motivators with strategic goals leads to higher retention, greater job satisfaction, and enhanced organizational outcomes.[51] When these intrinsic motivators align with the organization's mission, leaders feel more engaged, and their actions naturally resonate with their teams and stakeholders, fostering trust and a shared sense of purpose.[52,53]

CREATING A CULTURE OF ALIGNMENT

There are many other benefits to leading with this type of alignment. Researchers Roy Baumeister and Kathleen Vohs found that when personal values align with professional actions, leaders experience less decision fatigue.[54] This allows them to approach complex challenges with sharper focus and strategic thinking. Leaders driven by what truly motivates them are better equipped to adapt to change without losing sight of their core values—and during times of uncertainty or challenge, staying connected to core values becomes critical. Leaders who align their personal motivators with the organization's goals are more likely to view setbacks as opportunities for growth rather than insurmountable obstacles. This mindset reflects what Angela Duckworth writes about in her book *Grit:*

---

[51]   Deci, E. L., & Ryan, R. M. (1985). *Intrinsic motivation and self-determination in human behavior.* Springer.

[52]   Deci, E. L., & Ryan, R. M. (2000). The "what" and "why" of goal pursuits: Human needs and the self-determination of behavior. *Psychological Inquiry, 11*(4), 227–268. https://doi.org/10.1207/S15327965PLI1104_01

[53]   Pink, D. H. (2011). *Drive: The surprising truth about what motivates us.* Riverhead Books.

[54]   Baumeister, R. F., & Vohs, K. D. (2016). *Handbook of self-regulation: Research, theory, and applications* (3rd ed.). Guilford Press.

The Power of Passion and Perseverance, which are required for long-term success.[55]

By grounding their sense of purpose in the broader objectives of their organization, leaders can help themselves and their teams develop the stamina they need to remain focused and clear-headed for the long-term, even in the face of adversity.

There are no shortcuts. Cultures that prioritize alignment are shaped from the top down, not the other way around. This behavior must be demonstrated at the leadership level first. This is how high-performing teams are shaped and able to consistently achieve big goals.

Leaders who model this type of alignment create a ripple effect, first with their teams and then more broadly. Over time, their entire organization starts to change for the better. It sets the stage for a workplace where purpose and performance coexist, fostering greater collaboration and engagement. Amy Edmondson, the Novartis Professor of Leadership and Management at the Harvard Business School, conducts research on psychological safety, among other things. Her work highlights how alignment creates environments where people feel supported and inspired to bring their best selves to work.[56] Organizations that prioritize incentive alignment also have a competitive edge when it comes to attracting and retaining top talent.

---

[55] Duckworth, A. (2016). *Grit: The power of passion and perseverance.* Scribner.

[56] Edmondson, A. C. (2018). *The fearless organization: Creating psychological safety in the workplace for learning, innovation, and growth.* Wiley.

KEY TAKEAWAYS

High-performance leadership is seldom a consequence of effort, capability, or strategy alone. Rather, it emerges when leaders align personal motivational drivers with organizational goals. This provides the sustainable energy required to make good decisions, navigate challenges, and accelerate recovery after setbacks. This is not an aspirational ideal, but a key operational lever central to enduring achievement. Leaders who understand this and approach their work this way are more successful, as are their teams and companies.

How do you identify motivational drivers? The first step is an objective, personal audit of your motivational profile. Take time to help yourself and your team surface individual motivators, so generic incentives can be replaced with what really matters to you and your team. Such alignment reduces decision fatigue, elevates creativity, and strengthens execution velocity.

Introducing these practices across the organization completes the cycle. Purpose statements must inform budgeting, resource deployment, and performance reviews. Meetings should explicitly connect initiatives to their broader impact, while recognition programs ought to highlight behaviors that exemplify aligned values. Over time, this disciplined integration creates a culture that naturally nurtures and attracts talent whose values mirror the organization's own.

Leadership, at its core, is a sequence of choices that either bridge or widen the divide between strategic intent and meaningful action. By systematically anchoring every decision in clearly defined motivational drivers, both personal and collective, executives convert success from a transient numerical achievement into a sustainable model of purposeful impact.

- Leaders who align their actions with **intrinsic motivations** build resilience and foster deeper engagement, creating a foundation for long-term fulfillment and adaptability.

- **Purpose-driven motivation** empowers leaders to make thoughtful, values-based decisions, enabling them to navigate complexities with clarity and confidence.

- **Incentive alignment** connects personal motivations with organizational goals, driving meaningful leadership that inspires teams and cultivates a cohesive, purpose-driven culture.

CASE STUDY: NELSON MANDELA'S RESILIENT LEADERSHIP

Nelson Mandela's life and leadership journey exemplify the power of purpose-driven action in the face of immense adversity. His unwavering commitment to equality and justice didn't just define his character, it shaped his legacy as a leader and inspired a sociopolitical transformation in his homeland of South Africa—and around the world. Mandela's intrinsic motivation to dismantle apartheid and foster reconciliation was tested repeatedly during his twenty-seven years of imprisonment. Rather than allowing anger or despair to dominate his spirit, Mandela used his incarceration as a time for reflection and personal growth. He honed his ability to listen, strategize, and lead with empathy, recognizing that achieving his vision required not just defiance, but collaboration and understanding.[57]

---

[57] Carlin, J. (2008). *Playing the enemy: Nelson Mandela and the game that made a nation*. Penguin.

Mandela's release from prison in 1990 marked a pivotal moment for South Africa. At a time when the country was on the brink of civil war, Mandela's leadership offered a path of reconciliation rather than retribution. His ability to align his actions with his purpose was evident in his negotiations with the apartheid government, where he prioritized building a unified nation over seeking vengeance for past injustices. As South Africa's first Black president, Mandela continued to lead with humility and purpose. One of his most famous acts of reconciliation was his support for the national rugby team, the Springboks, during the 1995 Rugby World Cup. Despite the team being a symbol of apartheid for many Black South Africans, Mandela recognized the unifying potential of sports. Wearing the team's jersey and cap during the final match, he demonstrated his commitment to healing a divided nation. This act of purpose-driven leadership sent a powerful message of forgiveness and unity, helping to bridge deep racial divides.[58]

Mandela's intrinsic motivations were deeply tied to his vision of a fair and inclusive society. He consistently aligned his leadership actions with this purpose, even when it meant making personal sacrifices or facing criticism. His ability to balance resilience with humility transformed South Africa and inspired a global movement for justice and equality. His steadfast focus on creating a better future for all South Africans, coupled with his willingness to take bold, core-values-based actions, serves as a powerful model for leaders seeking to align their motivations with meaningful change.

Nelson Mandela's leadership journey demonstrates that staying true to your purpose, even in the face of immense challenges, can drive transformative change. His example reminds leaders

---

[58]   Stengel, R. (2009). *Mandela's way: Lessons on life, love, and courage*. Crown.

that aligning actions with values isn't just a personal choice—
it's a leadership imperative that builds trust, inspires others,
and creates lasting impact.

REFLECTION

Ask yourself the following questions and write your answers
in your journal. After, take time to reflect on your discoveries.

1. What are your core motivational drivers, and how do
   they shape your approach to leadership?

2. How aligned are your current goals and actions with
   your intrinsic motivations?

3. In what ways can you strengthen the alignment between
   your motivations and your leadership actions?

4. Reflect on a recent decision: Did it align with your
   core motivations, and how did that affect the outcome?

5. How can you foster an environment where both your
   team and you are motivated by purpose and aligned
   incentives?

SELF-AUDIT

Rate yourself on a scale from one to ten, where one means
"rarely or not at all" and ten means "frequently or very well."

1. I regularly reflect on my core motivations to ensure
   alignment with my leadership actions.

   1   2   3   4   5   6   7   8   9   10

2. My decisions are consistently driven by intrinsic
   motivators, rather than external validation.

   1   2   3   4   5   6   7   8   9   10

3. I actively seek to align my personal values with my organizational goals.

1   2   3   4   5   6   7   8   9   10

4. I am aware of how my motivations impact my leadership style and team dynamics.

1   2   3   4   5   6   7   8   9   10

5. My leadership actions reflect a clear sense of purpose and direction.

1   2   3   4   5   6   7   8   9   10

6. I prioritize long-term fulfillment over short-term rewards in my leadership approach.

1   2   3   4   5   6   7   8   9   10

7. I cultivate an environment where my team can connect their motivations with their roles.

1   2   3   4   5   6   7   8   9   10

8. I set goals that align with both my personal values and my professional responsibilities.

1   2   3   4   5   6   7   8   9   10

9. I feel a strong sense of purpose in my daily work.

1   2   3   4   5   6   7   8   9   10

10. I actively evaluate how my motivations shape my leadership style and impact my team's engagement.

1   2   3   4   5   6   7   8   9   10

EXERCISE: WRITE A MOTIVATION MISSION STATEMENT

Creating a Motivation Mission Statement is a powerful way to connect your core motivations to your leadership vision. This statement should reflect what drives you, align with your values, and serve as a guide for your professional journey. Start by identifying your primary motivational drivers. For example, a few of these might be commitment to innovation; passion for social impact; or a dedication to lifelong learning. Reflect on how these motivations shape your decisions, influence your leadership style, and guide your interactions with your team.

Once you've identified these drivers, craft a statement that encapsulates this alignment. Your Motivation Mission Statement will serve as a touchstone, helping you stay grounded in your values and make purpose-driven decisions, even in challenging situations. Revisit and refine your statement periodically to ensure it evolves as your motivations and professional circumstances change. Here are some examples of Motivation Mission Statements:

> Example 1: "My core motivation is to cultivate the next generation of leaders by fostering an environment of growth, mentorship, and empowerment. I believe that every leader's success is measured by the success of those they develop, and I am committed to providing my team with the guidance and opportunities to realize their full potential. By creating a culture that values learning, collaboration, and accountability, I aim to leave a legacy of strong, capable leaders who are equipped to lead with purpose and integrity."

> Example 2: "Driven by a passion for innovation and a commitment to lifelong learning, my mission is to lead with curiosity and resilience. I strive to create an environment that encourages creative problem-solving and values knowledge-sharing, enabling both personal and organizational growth. By fostering a culture of experimentation and adaptation, I aim to guide my team through challenges,

always learning and evolving to meet the demands of a rapidly changing world. This commitment to innovation and learning shapes my decisions and keeps our organization moving forward."

These examples demonstrate how a Motivation Mission Statement can articulate your values, connect with your leadership vision, and provide clarity for your actions. Use this exercise as an opportunity to clarify your motivations and link them to your professional objectives, creating a sustainable and purpose-driven approach to leadership.

COGNITIVE BIAS TRAPS

"We don't see things as they are; we see them as we are."

—Anais Nin

IN MY CAREER, there have been times when I was absolutely certain I was making the right decision, only to realize later that I missed something critical. I'm thinking about hiring decisions that didn't work out, strategies that seemed perfect on paper but fell apart during execution, or even conversations where I thought I communicated clearly, but the message didn't land. It's easy to chalk these mistakes up to circumstances or incomplete information, but more often than not, the culprit is cognitive bias. Let me share an example from my early career.

It was the 1990s and I was working at what was then Shearson Lehman Hutton. It was a crisp October afternoon, and my team was preparing for our annual national conference. We were all gathered in the thirty-ninth-floor conference room where the smell of strong coffee mingled with the equally strong smell of dry-erase markers sitting at the ready for the team's presentation. I'd been told that they had a fresh new approach for this year's conference and their excitement was palpable as everyone settled in for the presentation.

James, who was in his early thirties and always upbeat, stepped up to the front of the room.

"This is it," James had said with earnest enthusiasm, his fingertips tapping rhythmically on the team's conference report. His words resonated with a contagious certainty. "Our new approach is bold. It takes what worked last year and completely reinvents it. This year, we're not just hosting a conference—we're shaping the industry conversation." His colleagues clapped in support. "This year we have a plan to invite several new speakers and widen the scope of topics we typically cover. We also have some new technology we'll be using to bring in virtual presentations and better sound quality. It's time to refresh and broaden our content strategy for today's audience."

James looked confidently in my direction several times as he spoke, as did some of his colleagues, listening enthusiastically. Everyone knew that I was the ultimate decisionmaker, so when eyes weren't on James—with all his carefully prepared and visually engaging charts, projections, analyses, and project plan—they were on me. I tried to stay open and keep my expression positive, but my discomfort kept growing with every slide.

Things had worked so well last year, I thought. *Why the need for so much change?*

        DAVID L ZIMMERMAN, MSC, CPC

People—especially the bigwigs at Shearson I wanted to impress—had been happy with everything the way it already was. The entire team had enjoyed the accolades. Why reinvent the wheel? Why try to fix something that wasn't broken? My brain was telling me to play it safe, and I was having trouble focusing on James's ideas.

"Thanks for listening, everyone," James wrapped up, and then turned to me. "So, David, what are your thoughts?"

Everyone was staring at me with similar enthusiastic-but-anxious expressions. I took a deep breath to steady my thoughts.

"James, great presentation. Much appreciated. Thank you. But listen, guys . . ." I paused, trying to carefully select my next words. I decided to be completely honest. "I don't understand why we would want to mess with something that has been working so well."

And with those words, the air went out of the room as fast as a deflating balloon.

The body language of every single person in the conference room shifted from excitement to complete resignation. I didn't realize it as I spoke, but it was a defining moment for me and my team. The conference would remain the same; I got my way, but at a cost. From that moment forward, everyone followed the script. They did what they were supposed to do to get the job done, but their excitement and enthusiasm plummeted.

By playing it safe, I'd won the battle but lost the war. I'd opted for the familiar over the innovative. I'd steered away from the risk inherent in creating something new, and in doing so, I had disappointed my team. In hindsight, their approach would have been just as good, if not better. Why? Because they were focused on impressing Shearson's evolving audience, and I was focused on impressing my bosses—who, just like me, didn't like change. Confirmation bias had crept in, and I took the bait. I just didn't notice it in the moment.

Months later, as I stood backstage watching a nearly identical conference program from the previous year unfold, I couldn't help but notice that my team's enthusiasm was professional but muted. I felt a sinking sensation in my stomach. While the applause still came, the audience's response lacked the spontaneous vigor of the year before. The conversations afterward felt rehearsed—obligatory rather than energized. It was clear that what was once groundbreaking had become expected. I should have listened to my team. I should have trusted their ideas. We should have innovated, as they had suggested. Unintentionally, I'd favored the information that aligned with what I already believed, while overlooking alternative perspectives that could have led to a better decision and outcomes. In so doing, I also missed an important opportunity to support and work more closely with my team. I fell into natural and safe patterns that year; and thirty years later, I still regret it.

The truth is our biases aren't obvious. These mental shortcuts quietly influence how we interpret information, assess risk, and even interact with others. A bias is a prejudice or inclination towards something. It can be either or positive or negative. A cognitive bias, on the other hand, is a specific type of bias that involves an error in thinking or reasoning. These biases are often unconscious and can affect how we perceive information, make decisions, and form judgments. As leaders, we face both of these biases daily. They inform our decisions in ways we don't always recognize. While they're not inherently bad (they do, after all, help us process the world faster), unchecked biases can narrow our thinking, derail our judgment, and create blind spots that limit our leadership potential and the growth of our teams. So, let's explore how common biases sneak into our leadership, show up in decision-making, and impact our teams and organization. More importantly, we'll dive into practical tools and strategies to recognize and counteract these biases. The goal isn't to eliminate them: that's impossible. Instead, it's to sharpen your awareness, challenge your assumptions, and lead with clarity and balance.

IDENTIFYING YOUR COGNITIVE BIASES

Decision-making as a leader is complicated. You've got limited time, competing priorities, and plenty of pressure. It's no wonder our brains take shortcuts to help us keep up. But here's the catch: those shortcuts, known to behavioral psychologists as cognitive biases, can quietly derail your objectivity, affect team dynamics, and even block innovation. Everyone has cognitive biases. They are part of our evolutionary wiring. We couldn't get through the day without them. Researchers estimate that the average adult makes on the order of 35,000 conscious decisions each day, spanning everything from trivial to high-stakes choices. Cognitive biases help us process information quickly, so we aren't overwhelmed and can function efficiently. But these shortcuts can also mislead, so as leaders we need to be equipped to recognize and manage our cognitive biases, so they don't cause problems. Here are the ten most common leadership biases:

1. **Confirmation Bias:** This happens when you gravitate toward information that supports what you already believe while ignoring anything that challenges that belief. It's like having a built-in filter that only lets in what feels comfortable. For leaders, this can be dangerous. Let's say you're rolling out a new initiative, and you're convinced it's the right move. Confirmation bias might lead you to only look at data that supports your approach while overlooking risks or alternative

perspectives.[59] The result? You miss out on opportunities to innovate or improve because you're reinforcing old patterns instead of exploring new ones.

2. **Anchoring Bias:** This is when the first piece of information you receive sticks with you and influences everything that comes after. Think about a budget meeting where someone throws out an initial number. It's hard not to let that figure shape the rest of the discussion, even if better information becomes available later. This bias is especially common in goal-setting, strategic planning, and negotiations. To combat anchoring bias, leaders need to actively question first impressions and encourage teams to bring fresh perspectives to the table.

3. **Outcome Bias:** This one is especially sneaky. Outcome bias happens when you judge a decision solely by its result instead of evaluating the quality of the decision-making process. For example, if a risky move pays off, you might call it a great decision even if it was based on flawed reasoning.[59] The danger here is that this bias can lead to overconfidence in strategies that worked by luck, not design. Leaders who focus on process rather than just outcomes are better positioned to learn from their successes and failures.

4. **Overconfidence Bias:** Leaders often feel like they need to have all the answers. Overconfidence bias happens when you overestimate your knowledge or abilities, leading to risky decisions or missed opportunities to

---

[59] Effectiviology. (2021, May 6). Outcome bias: The problematic effect of judging decisions based on their outcomes. *Effectiviology. https://effectiviology.com/outcome-bias/*

gather feedback.[60] This bias can show up when tackling complex problems alone, assuming your insights are enough without seeking input from others. The fix? Stay humble. Acknowledge that collaboration often leads to better results.

5. **Blind Spot Bias:** This is a classic leadership pitfall. Blind spot bias is when you can easily spot cognitive biases in others but struggle to see them in yourself.[61] Leaders who think they're immune to bias are overlooking areas in critical need of personal growth. The solution? Make self-reflection a regular habit. Ask for feedback from your team and be willing to examine your own assumptions.

6. **Availability Heuristic:** This is when decisions are based on the information that's easiest to recall, rather than the most relevant data. For instance, a recent customer complaint might loom larger in your mind than months of positive feedback, skewing your judgment.[62] This bias often leads to reactive decisions that address immediate concerns while neglecting long-term

---

[60] Nickerson, R. S. (1998). Confirmation bias: A ubiquitous phenomenon in many guises. Review of General Psychology, 2(2), 175-220. *https://www.doi.org/10.1037/1089-2680.2.2.175*

[60] Moore, D. A., & Healy, P. J. (2008). The trouble with overconfidence. *Psychological Review, 115*(2), 502–517. https://doi.org/10.1037/0033-295X.115.2.502

[61] Pronin, E., Lin, D. Y., & Ross, L. (2002). The bias blind spot: Perceptions of bias in self versus others. *Personality and Social Psychology Bulletin, 28*(3), 369–381. https://doi.org/10.1177/0146167202286008

[62] Tversky, A., & Kahneman, D. (1973). Availability: A heuristic for judging frequency and probability. *Cognitive Psychology, 5*(2), 207–232. https://doi.org/10.1016/0010-0285(73)90033-9

priorities. To counter this, leaders need to step back and evaluate the full picture before making a move.

7. **Groupthink:** This happens when team members prioritize agreement over critical analysis, often to maintain harmony.[63] While this approach might feel good in the moment, this bias can stifle innovation and discourage people from voicing dissenting opinions. Great leaders create a culture where it's safe to challenge ideas—so, encourage debate, and make it clear that disagreement is not just welcome, but essential for the team's success.

8. **Bandwagon Bias:** Similar to groupthink, bandwagon bias is when leaders or team members adopt ideas simply because they're popular, rather than assessing their actual value.[64] For example, you might jump on a trend in your industry because everyone else is doing it, only to find that it doesn't fit your organization's needs. Avoid this by asking tough questions like, "Does this align with our goals?" or "Are we doing this because it's right for us, or because it's what everyone else is doing?"

9. **Hyperbolic Discounting:** This is the tendency to prefer immediate rewards over larger future payoffs, even when waiting would yield objectively greater value.

10. **Status Quo Bias:** This bias is characterized by a preference for how things already are, and a general resistance

---

[63] Janis, I. L. (1972). *Victims of groupthink: A psychological study of foreign-policy decisions and fiascoes.* Houghton Mifflin.

[64] Asch, S. E. (1955). Opinions and social pressure. *Scientific American, 193*(5), 31–35. https://doi.org/10.1038/scientificamerican1155-31

to change—even when there are better alternatives to the current method of doing things.

Maybe seeing this list has already helped you recognize some of your cognitive biases. Remember, we all have them; so, denial is useless and counterproductive. But if you are willing to identify your biases and manage them effectively, that can yield significant benefits and advantages to you as a leader.

MANAGING COGNITIVE BIASES

How often do you stop and think about the mental shortcuts your brain takes when you are making a decision? If you're like most of us, the answer is probably "not enough" or "never," and that's how cognitive biases can quietly wreak havoc on our leadership style. One of the core principles of effective leadership is learning to recognize and manage these biases. Why? Because as leaders, our decisions don't just impact us on an individual level, they impact our teams, department strategies, and even the broader goals of the organization that employs us. When biases sneak into our decision-making, they can steer us off course. Israeli-American Psychologist and Nobel Laureate Daniel Kahneman, author of the bestselling book, *Thinking Fast and Slow*, explains that our biases often work in the background, influencing our judgment without us even realizing it.[65] He stresses the importance of reflection and self-awareness as tools to uncover these hidden influences. It's about taking the time to pause and ask, "Is my decision rooted in fact, or am I being led by an assumption I haven't even questioned?"

---

[65]   Kahneman, D. (2011). *Thinking, fast and slow.* Farrar, Straus and Giroux.

Bias Mapping is a structured reflection process where you revisit past leadership moments with the intention of characterizing your decision-making style, pinpointing patterns, and identifying where biases tend to creep into your process. Here's how it works: Consider a few key leadership moments when you think your choices may have been influenced by certain biases. Were you overly swayed by the first idea in a meeting? This might be anchoring bias. Did you dismiss feedback that didn't align with your initial thinking? This could be confirmation bias. By reflecting on past behaviors, you start to see patterns and can develop strategies to approach future decisions with more clarity and objectivity.[66]

The insights you uncover during Bias Mapping tie directly into the two thinking systems that we use to make decisions.[67] Kahneman describes these systems in his work. System 1 is your brain's fast, intuitive mode of thinking. It's great for making quick judgments, but is where most biases live. System 2 is slower and more deliberate—the kind of thinking you need for complex decision-making.[68]

Bias Mapping helps you shift from System 1 to System 2 when it matters most. It guides you away from gut reactions and toward more intentional, well-considered choices. Researchers Richard Thaler and Cass Sunstein, in their work on decision-making, show that structured frameworks like Bias Mapping improve decision quality by replacing automatic

---

[66] Bazerman, M. H., & Moore, D. A. (2012). *Judgment in managerial decision making* (8th ed.). Wiley.

[67] Kahneman, D. (2011). *Thinking, fast and slow.* Farrar, Straus and Giroux.

[68] Kahneman, D. (2011). *Thinking, fast and slow.* Farrar, Straus and Giroux.

responses with intentional thought.[69] This approach doesn't just help you recognize your biases—it gives you tools to systematically address them, moving you from *reactive* to *proactive* decision-making.

Once you have identified your biases, it's easier to create a system for actively managing them. That's where behavioral researcher and author, Max H. Bazerman, and Professor Don Moore, the Lorraine Tyson Mitchell Chair in Leadership and Communication at the Haas School of Business at UC Berkeley, come in with their concept of Bias Checks.[70] Think of these as deliberate moments within your decision-making process where you hit the pause button and ask yourself some tough questions, like: "What assumptions am I making here?" "Am I overlooking perspectives that don't align with my initial view?" "Does this decision reflect my team's diverse input, or just my own instincts?" Bias Checks are simple but powerful. They force you to take a step back and ensure your decisions align with organizational goals and the input of others. By building these pauses into your decision-making process, you don't just reduce bias, you also set the tone for a culture of thoughtful, intentional, and inclusive leadership. Recognizing and managing cognitive biases isn't a one-and-done exercise. Like many of the behaviors we've discussed in *The Juncture Code*, this is a discipline that you must develop, practice, and model for your people. When you take the time to pause, reflect, and challenge your assumptions, you're not just making better decisions, you're showing your team how to think critically and consider diverse viewpoints.

---

[69]   Thaler, R. H., & Sunstein, C. R. (2008). *Nudge: Improving decisions about health, wealth, and happiness.* Yale University Press.

[70]   Bazerman, M. H., & Moore, D. A. (2012). *Judgment in managerial decision making* (8th ed.). Wiley.

KEY TAKEAWAYS

As we've explored, cognitive biases are a natural part of how we think. They play an important role in every decision we make. Our unique personalities, upbringings, and experiences shape who we are, including our biases. We can't dismiss them—but we can't let them hold us back, either. Understanding your biases is the first step in learning to manage them. Bias Mapping and Bias Checks help you build that awareness and manage your biases in the crucial moments of your day. The more intentional you become about recognizing and addressing your biases, the more balanced and inclusive your decision-making process will become. This evolution in your thinking doesn't just benefit you, it strengthens your team and positions your organization for growth.

- Unchecked cognitive biases limit objectivity and hinder innovation. Recognizing and managing biases is critical for leaders to make balanced and effective decisions.

- Bias Mapping provides a systematic approach to improving decision-making. By identifying patterns, triggers, and strategies to manage biases, leaders move from reactive to intentional decision-making, fostering clarity and alignment with goals.

- Leaders who actively challenge assumptions and seek diverse perspectives create stronger, more inclusive teams. Intentional processes to counter your biases, like Bias Checks, will empower you to balance stability and adaptability, building a culture of innovation and trust.

CASE STUDY: STEVE JOBS' JOURNEY TO INCLUSIVE INNOVATION

His story is legendary. Despite his visionary genius, Steve Jobs was not a perfect leader. Early in his career, his leadership style revealed confirmation bias. He often sought out ideas that validated his own beliefs while dismissing those that didn't. This limited collaboration strained professional relationships, deterred innovation, and ultimately contributed to his removal as Apple's CEO in 1985.[71] During his time away from Apple, Jobs founded NeXT and became heavily involved with Pixar, two experiences that profoundly shaped his perspective. At NeXT, he faced setbacks that forced him to confront the limitations of his rigid decision-making style. Meanwhile, at Pixar, Jobs witnessed the power of collective creativity and the importance of diverse inputs. These experiences transformed his leadership style.

When Jobs returned to Apple in 1997, his leadership reflected a deeper commitment to minimizing his biases. Jobs actively sought out differing perspectives and fostered an environment where his team felt empowered to challenge his ideas. This openness helped drive Apple's resurgence and its culture of innovation, culminating in iconic products like the iMac, iPod, and iPhone.[72] Jobs took deliberate steps to challenge his initial assumptions and practice iterative refinement. Additionally, he began relying heavily on user feedback and rigorous product testing to ensure that decisions were informed by broader insights rather than reactive impulses.[73]

---

[71] Isaacson, W. (2011). *Steve Jobs*. Simon & Schuster.
[72] Isaacson, W. (2011). *Steve Jobs*. Simon & Schuster.
[73] Kahneman, D. (2011). *Thinking, fast and slow*. Farrar, Straus and Giroux.

The development of the iPhone stands as a testament to Jobs's evolved leadership approach. By creating a culture that valued diverse viewpoints and collaborative problem-solving, Jobs turned Apple into one of the world's most innovative and valuable companies. As the late Edgar Henry Schein highlighted in his writings, leaders who recognize their biases and work to overcome them build environments that thrive on creativity and adaptability.[74]

Jobs serves as a powerful example of how addressing cognitive biases doesn't just improve individual decision-making, it transforms organizations. His journey underscores the importance of reflection, openness, and deliberate action in creating resilient, high-performing teams.

REFLECTION

Ask yourself the following questions and write your answers in your journal. After, take time to reflect on your discoveries.

1. Can you identify your personal biases?

2. Do you actively challenge your assumptions?

3. Are you open to diverse feedback?

4. Have you ever done Bias Mapping?

5. Are you willing to use Bias Checks?

SELF-AUDIT

Rate yourself on a scale from one to ten, where one means "rarely or not at all" and ten means "frequently or very well."

---

[74] Schein, E. H. (2010). *Organizational culture and leadership* (4th ed.). Jossey-Bass.

1. I regularly question my assumptions when making decisions.

     1   2   3   4   5   6   7   8   9   10

2. I actively seek feedback from those with differing perspectives.

     1   2   3   4   5   6   7   8   9   10

3. I am aware of cognitive biases and their effects on decision-making.

     1   2   3   4   5   6   7   8   9   10

4. I take steps to pause and examine potential biases in critical decisions.

     1   2   3   4   5   6   7   8   9   10

5. I track decision-making processes to identify patterns of bias.

     1   2   3   4   5   6   7   8   9   10

6. I remain open to perspectives that challenge my beliefs.

     1   2   3   4   5   6   7   8   9   10

7. I reflect on past decisions to understand how biases played a role.

     1   2   3   4   5   6   7   8   9   10

8. I engage in discussions with diverse thinkers to broaden my perspective.

     1   2   3   4   5   6   7   8   9   10

9. I am committed to managing cognitive biases in my leadership.

     1   2   3   4   5   6   7   8   9   10

10. I view awareness of biases as integral to effective decision-making.

     1   2   3   4   5   6   7   8   9   10

EXERCISE: DISCOVER YOUR DECISION-MAKING BIASES

Take fifteen minutes to reflect on recent decisions you've made in your leadership role—and remember that this isn't about judgment, it's about discovery. Think of it as an opportunity to uncover how cognitive biases might be influencing your choices and explore what you could do differently in the future. In your journal, write down the following steps:

1. **Identify a Recent Decision:** Start by choosing a decision you made recently. It could be something small, like a team assignment, or something larger, like setting a strategic goal.

2. **Examine Potential Biases:** Reflect on the decision-making process. Did any cognitive biases, such as confirmation bias, anchoring bias, or availability heuristic, play a role? Were there moments when your assumptions went unchallenged or when a single perspective dominated your thinking?

3. **Reimagine Your Decision:** Now, think about how the outcome might have been different if you had approached the decision with a more open or intentional mindset. What would have changed if you had questioned your initial assumptions or actively sought diverse viewpoints?

4. **Capture Insights:** Write down what you learned from this reflection. Consider how these insights might help you approach future decisions with greater clarity, objectivity, and inclusivity.

CHAPTER 6

THE SILENT INFLUENCER

*"We all have implicit biases. What matters is what
we do when we recognize them."*

—Verna Myers

I'LL NEVER FORGET a moment in my leadership career at Wells Fargo that taught me how impactful implicit bias can be. I was interviewing two candidates for the senior sales leadership role on my team. Both were exceptionally qualified, with impressive track records and glowing recommendations. On paper, they were equals. But as I reviewed my notes later that afternoon, I realized that I had described one candidate as "confident and assertive" and the other as "aggressive and overly ambitious." Seeing the difference in these two descriptions in black and white next to each other hit me like a ton of bricks. Their qualifications were nearly identical, yet I had framed them completely differently in my mind. Looking closer, I realized the candidate I'd called "confident" reminded me of someone I had mentored years earlier: similar tone, similar background, even a similar way of answering questions. That familiarity made me feel comfortable, and I mistook that comfort for more competence and likely a better fit. The other candidate had a different style: more direct, more intense. Because that did not match my norm, I unfairly raised red flags.

As I reflected on my initial reactions, I saw how my unconscious perceptions were shaping my judgment. The "confident" candidate aligned more with my own leadership style, and I had subconsciously favored this person because they felt familiar. The candidate that I had labeled as "aggressive," on the other hand, had a different energy—one I wasn't personally used to working with, so I'd labeled that difference negatively. The point is: neither label was fair or accurate. They were simply products of my implicit biases quietly influencing how I evaluated two talented professionals.

Implicit bias, also known as unconscious bias, refer to the automatic and unintentional attitudes, stereotypes, or beliefs that impact our understanding, actions, and decisions. Recognizing this in myself became a humbling moment—and a turning point. I realized that if I wasn't intentional about confronting my own implicit biases, they could compromise not only my decision-making, but also the culture I wanted to build: one of inclusion, fairness, and growth that would ultimately strengthen the organization. That experience became a lesson in pausing to question my instincts, seeking diverse perspectives, and creating processes that checked my blind spots.[75]

[75] Eastern Washington University Libraries. (2022, January 23). Implicit bias: Library resources. Eastern Washington University. *https://www.research.ewu.edu/implicit-bias*

    DAVID L ZIMMERMAN, MSC, CPC

RECOGNIZING IMPLICIT BIAS

Because implicit bias is not overt or deliberate, it is challenging to spot. Like most biases, it operates in the background, shaping how we perceive others based on factors like gender, race, age, or even personality traits. It's the subtle but powerful force that can undermine our objectivity and limit the potential of our teams if left unchecked. Researchers Mahzarin Banaji and Anthony Greenwald, who developed the Implicit Association Test (IAT), show that implicit bias can distort decisions in ways we're not even aware of, from hiring and promotions to team dynamics and conflict resolution.[75]

Working quietly behind the scenes, implicit biases subtly influence how we make decisions. Our biases shape recruitment choices, promotions, and even team dynamics in ways we don't always notice. While a bias may seem small or insignificant to you, its impact can be far-reaching, creating barriers to inclusivity in the workplace. The good news is that understanding your biases is the first step toward addressing them. When leaders take the time to recognize how the assumptions that show up in their decisions, they can develop strategies to counteract them. In the last chapter, we discussed ten common biases that leaders face. Here are a few additional biases and how they can be addressed.

Role-Based Bias

Role-based bias occurs when leaders make assumptions about someone's abilities based solely on stereotypes tied to certain roles. For example, technical jobs might be unconsciously associated with specific demographics, while caregiving roles

---

[75]   Not sure of original citation number (was also in Chapter 6 in original manuscript and reference doc.)

might be linked to others. These assumptions can lead leaders to overlook qualified candidates who don't fit those stereotypes. A study by Madeline Heilman found that these role-based assumptions often limit diversity in fields like engineering and nursing.[76] To counter this, leaders can focus on skills and qualifications in job descriptions rather than relying on past norms or demographic assumptions. Asking questions that are rooted in objectivity, rather than defaulting to stereotypes, is a great start. For example, in a hiring situation, avoid asking questions like, "What type of person would be the best candidate for this job?" and instead ask, "What does this role *really* require?"

Appearance Bias

Appearance bias happens when judgments are made based on how someone looks rather than their actual abilities. This might include assumptions based on clothing, grooming, or physical traits. Research shows that people who fit traditional standards of "professional appearance" are often perceived as more competent, even if their skills don't align.[77] For leaders, this bias can lead to favoring individuals who "look the part" over those who truly excel. To address this, focus on measurable performance indicators rather than outward presentation. Regularly remind yourself: competence isn't about appearance, it's about results.

---

[76] Kahneman, D. (2011). *Thinking, fast and slow.* Farrar, Straus and Giroux.

[77] Tett, R. P., & Simonet, D. V. (2011). Appearance and leadership effectiveness: An empirical investigation. *Journal of Applied Psychology, 96*(5), 967–981. https://doi.org/10.1037/a0024345

Affinity Bias

Also known as similarity bias, affinity bias occurs when we gravitate toward people who share our backgrounds, interests, or experiences. While shared connections can build rapport, they can also create blind spots. For example, a leader might favor someone who went to the same university or shares a hobby, unintentionally sidelining others with diverse perspectives. Anthony Greenwald and Thomas Pettigrew highlighted how affinity bias can limit diversity and innovation.[78] To counter this, leaders can make a conscious effort to engage with team members who think differently or bring unique experiences to the table. Asking for input from a variety of voices ensures decisions reflect a broader perspective.

Stereotype Bias

Stereotype bias involves generalized beliefs about certain groups, such as assumptions based on gender, race, age, or ethnicity. For instance, a leader might assume younger employees are more tech-savvy or that older employees are less adaptable. These assumptions can lead to unequal opportunities and create unnecessary barriers. Claude Steele found that stereotype threat can even affect how individuals see themselves, impacting their performance if they feel they're being judged based on group stereotypes.[79] Leaders can challenge these biases by focusing on individuals' unique

---

[78] Greenwald, A. G., & Pettigrew, T. F. (2014). With malice toward none and charity for some: Ingroup favoritism enables discrimination. *American Psychologist, 69*(7), 669–684. https://doi.org/10.1037/a0036056

[79] Steele, C. M. (2010). *Whistling Vivaldi: And other clues to how stereotypes affect us.* W.W. Norton.

strengths and taking time to reflect on whether stereotypes are influencing their decisions.

The Halo/Horns Effect

This bias occurs when a single positive or negative trait disproportionately influences how a leader views someone's overall abilities. For example, a team member who excels in one area might be assumed to excel across the board (halo effect), while someone who struggles in one task might be unfairly labeled as incompetent (horns effect). Edward Thorndike described how these biases skew evaluations, making it harder to give balanced feedback.[80] Leaders can mitigate the halo/horns effect by using structured evaluations that focus on specific, measurable outcomes. This ensures a more objective view of performance.

Do you recognize any of these implicit biases? Bias awareness is the first step. But true leadership means taking action to identify, challenge, and overcome these biases to create an environment where everyone can thrive.

COUNTERING IMPLICIT BIAS

Purdue Researchers and Professors John F. Dovidio and Samuel L Gaertner found that leaders who actively work to identify and address their biases lay the foundation for stronger engagement and trust within their teams.[81] Creating a bias-

---

[80] Thorndike, E. L. (1920). A constant error in psychological ratings. *Journal of Applied Psychology, 4*(1), 25–29. https://doi.org/10.1037/h0071663

[81] Dovidio, J. F., & Gaertner, S. L. (2004). Aversive racism. In M. P. Zanna (Ed.), *Advances in experimental social psychology* (Vol. 36, pp. 1–52). Academic Press.

aware mindset and culture doesn't happen by accident—it takes intentional effort. Leaders need to make bias awareness, reflection, and adaptation part of their work routine, regularly examining how biases might be influencing their decisions and incorporating disciplines to stop these negative patterns. This chapter introduces the Conscious Calibration technique, a practical approach designed to help leaders recognize bias in the moment and take corrective action. By consistently applying this technique, leaders can create a workplace culture that prioritizes fairness.

Conscious Calibration is a practical approach that helps leaders identify and address implicit biases in their decision-making. It's about making periodic reflection and recalibration a habit, enabling leaders to recognize how their unconscious biases might be shaping their actions. By actively engaging in self-assessment and seeking feedback from team members with diverse perspectives, leaders can refine their understanding of bias and take meaningful steps to counteract its effects. This isn't a one-time fix; it's an ongoing process that ensures leaders remain responsive to the complexities of workplace dynamics and aware of the biases that may arise. The Conscious Calibration framework offers leaders three key practices:

1. **Self-Reflect Regularly:** Take intentional time to examine personal biases and how they may influence your decisions. Consider both your own experiences and the expectations tied to your leadership role.

2. **Seek Diverse Input:** Actively invite feedback from team members with different backgrounds and perspectives to broaden your understanding and uncover blind spots.

3. **Challenge Assumptions Actively:** Avoid defaulting to snap judgments. Instead, question your initial reactions and explore alternative viewpoints to ensure decisions are fair and well-informed.

Research on stereotypes and bias by Social Psychologist and Emeritus Professor at Stanford University Claude Steele highlights the power of self-awareness and intentional recalibration in creating inclusive environments.[82] Conscious Calibration aligns with this research, equipping leaders with tools to engage in reflective practices and make equitable decisions. By integrating these habits into their leadership, leaders can foster stronger trust, enhance team dynamics, and cultivate a workplace where everyone feels valued. When leaders commit to identifying and addressing bias, they build stronger teams, foster trust, and create environments where individuals are valued for their unique contributions. By staying curious, open, and reflective, leaders can navigate the complexities of implicit bias and lead with greater fairness and authenticity.

KEY TAKEAWAYS

Implicit bias is a silent partner in every decision we make at work and beyond. Left unexamined, these mental shortcuts can quietly steer hiring choices, performance reviews, and culturebuilding efforts away from the fairness and inclusion we seek. My own experience at Wells Fargo underscored that bias is not a moral failing; it is a universal human tendency. What distinguishes effective leaders is their willingness to surface these hidden influences and recalibrate before they distort outcomes.

---

[82] Steele, C. M. (2010). *Whistling Vivaldi: And other clues to how stereotypes affect us.* W.W. Norton.

Conscious Calibration provides a practical path forward. By pausing to reflect, soliciting perspectives different from our own, and actively challenging first impressions, we convert bias from an unseen liability into an opportunity for intentional leadership. These habits require discipline, yet they are neither complex nor timeconsuming. Five minutes of reflection after a meeting, a quick request for a contrary viewpoint, or a structured checklist before a promotion discussion can be enough to interrupt the bias cycle.

This is not a "check the box" exercise. Bias awareness must become as routine as reviewing financial statements or monitoring key performance indicators. When fairness is treated as a strategic metric—tracked, discussed, and improved—trust deepens, innovation flourishes, and performance follows. Teams feel recognized for their capabilities rather than their conformity, and the organization gains a competitive edge by unlocking the full spectrum of its talent.

As you move forward, resist the urge to delegate this work to HR or a yearly workshop. Make it personal, make it daily, and make it visible. Your example will signal that inclusivity is not an initiative—it is a leadership standard. In doing so, you will not only mitigate risk, but you will model the clarity, courage, and inclusiveness that define exceptional decisionmakers.

- Leaders who actively identify and address implicit biases create more inclusive teams, fostering trust, engagement, and collaboration.

- Conscious Calibration provides a practical framework for recognizing biases, reflecting on their impact, and taking corrective action in real-time.

- Addressing implicit biases in leadership decisions builds a fairer, more equitable workplace, strengthening organizational culture and performance.

CASE STUDY: KEN FRAZIER'S BLUEPRINT FOR INCLUSIVE LEADERSHIP

Ken Frazier's leadership at pharmaceutical giant Merck is a powerful example of how addressing implicit bias can transform an organization's culture. As one of the few Black CEOs of a Fortune 500 company, Frazier has faced and overcome countless biases throughout his career. His path to the C-Suite was shaped by personal and professional challenges. Raised by a single father in inner-city Philadelphia, he experienced discrimination firsthand. These experiences inspired his commitment to creating fairer, more inclusive workplaces. After earning his degree from Harvard Law School, Frazier joined Merck in 1992, working his way up to CEO in 2011. Along the way, he developed a deep understanding of how biases, often unconscious, can influence decisions at every level of an organization.[83] But Frazier didn't just stop at navigating these challenges himself; he made it his mission to confront and minimize bias across Merck, especially in areas like hiring, promotions, and team dynamics. His efforts offer a practical roadmap for leaders who want to embed inclusivity into their organizations. Recognizing that systemic inequities are often baked into corporate structures, he prioritized confronting these biases head-on. He understood that unconscious bias doesn't just hinder individual growth—it affects the entire organization by limiting diversity, innovation, and overall effectiveness. Drawing from his own experiences and insights, he championed changes that addressed the root causes of

---

[83] Hymowitz, C. (2012). Breaking the mold: Ken Frazier's journey from law to leadership at Merck. *The Wall Street Journal.*

inequality, from biased hiring practices to subjective performance evaluations.[84]

To address these challenges, Frazier implemented what can be seen as an organizational version of Conscious Calibration. He led efforts to regularly review company policies, focusing on identifying and eliminating biases that might otherwise go unnoticed. Managers and executives were encouraged to participate in bias training. This approach mirrors social science research showing that ongoing reflection and recalibration are essential for disrupting biases and creating fairer workplaces.[85]

One of Frazier's standout initiatives was introducing objective, merit-based evaluation systems. By emphasizing measurable competencies and accomplishments over subjective assessments, he shifted the company's focus to what employees could do, rather than who they were or how they looked. This helped counteract biases like affinity bias and confirmation bias, creating a more level playing field for all employees.[86] Frazier's efforts also included specific policies aimed at dismantling systemic biases:

- **Blind Resume Reviews:** Removing personal information like names and educational backgrounds to reduce biases tied to race, gender, or pedigree.

---

[84]   Baker, M., & Shelly, J. (2019). *Ken Frazier's legacy of leadership: Equity, inclusion, and merit-based advancement at Merck.* Harvard Business Review.

[85]   Dovidio, J. F., & Gaertner, S. L. (2004). Aversive racism. In M. P. Zanna (Ed.), *Advances in experimental social psychology* (Vol. 36, pp. 1–52). Academic Press.

[86]   Banaji, M. R., & Greenwald, A. G. (2016). *Blindspot: Hidden biases of good people.* Bantam.

- **Inclusive Leadership Development Programs:** Mentorship and training initiatives designed to create opportunities for underrepresented groups, helping to diversify Merck's leadership pipeline.[87]

- **Objective Performance Metrics:** Standardizing how performance was evaluated, ensuring that metrics were tied to measurable outcomes rather than subjective impressions.

These initiatives didn't just make Merck more equitable; they also made it more effective. His commitment to inclusivity fostered higher employee engagement, which research links to improved retention, productivity, and team morale.[88] His leadership proved that fairness and inclusion aren't just moral imperatives—they are a strategic advantage. Frazier's influence extends beyond Merck. As a vocal advocate for corporate responsibility, he's inspired other leaders to reexamine their own practices and prioritize inclusivity as a core business principle. By embedding fairness into Merck's policies and culture, he demonstrated how Conscious Calibration can drive meaningful change on both organizational and societal levels.

Ken Frazier's leadership demonstrates that creating an inclusive, equitable organization is not only the right thing to do, but also a strategic advantage. His story reminds leaders that dismantling bias and fostering inclusivity requires ongoing effort, courage, and a commitment to purpose. Leaders who follow

---

[87]   Merck. (2018). *Annual report on diversity and inclusion.* Merck & Co., Inc.

[88]   Harter, J. K., Schmidt, F. L., & Hayes, T. L. (2002). Business-unit-level relationship between employee satisfaction, employee engagement, and business outcomes: A meta-analysis. *Journal of Applied Psychology, 87*(2), 268–279. https://doi.org/10.1037/0021-9010.87.2.268

Frazier's example will be well-equipped to drive meaningful, lasting transformation within their teams and organizations.

REFLECTION

Ask yourself the following questions and write your answers in your journal. After, take time to reflect on your discoveries.

1. In what ways might implicit biases affect your leadership decisions and interactions?

2. What strategies, such as Conscious Calibration, can help you identify and address stereotypes affecting your team dynamics?

3. Can you identify any role-based or appearance-based biases in your leadership expectations, and how might they impact your team's performance or development?

4. How does your current decision-making approach include diverse perspectives?

5. What specific actions or policies can you implement to build a more inclusive and bias-aware culture within your team?

SELF-AUDIT

Rate yourself on a scale from one to ten, where one means "rarely or not at all" and ten means "frequently or very well."

1. I actively seek to identify and address my own implicit biases through regular reflection and self-assessment.

    1   2   3   4   5   6   7   8   9   10

2. I encourage open and constructive discussions about bias and inclusivity within my team, fostering a safe space for dialogue.

1   2   3   4   5   6   7   8   9   10

3. I regularly evaluate my expectations of team members to ensure they are based on performance and potential, not stereotypes.

1   2   3   4   5   6   7   8   9   10

4. I actively seek diverse perspectives from my team to inform my decisions and challenge my own assumptions.

1   2   3   4   5   6   7   8   9   10

5. I consciously question assumptions or judgments that may stem from role-based or appearance-based stereotypes.

1   2   3   4   5   6   7   8   9   10

6. I recognize how my own background and experiences influence my leadership style and decision-making.

1   2   3   4   5   6   7   8   9   10

7. I welcome and act on feedback from colleagues or team members regarding any biases I may exhibit.

1   2   3   4   5   6   7   8   9   10

8. I strive to create a team culture where diversity and inclusivity are valued, celebrated, and embedded into daily practices.

1   2   3   4   5   6   7   8   9   10

9. I avoid making snap judgments based on appearance or background and instead focus on measurable contributions.

1   2   3   4   5   6   7   8   9   10

    DAVID L ZIMMERMAN, MSC, CPC

10. I take consistent steps to educate myself about biases and inclusivity practices relevant to my leadership and industry.

1   2   3   4   5   6   7   8   9   10

EXERCISE: CONDUCT A BIAS AWARENESS DAY

A Bias Awareness Day is an opportunity to intentionally observe how biases, whether implicit or explicit, might influence your interactions, decisions, or leadership style. By dedicating time to reflect, document, and strategize, you can uncover patterns and take actionable steps to address these biases. This exercise aligns perfectly with the Conscious Calibration framework, helping you build a bias-aware mindset that promotes inclusivity in your leadership.

Here's a practical, conversational guide to conducting a Bias Awareness Day:

1. **Start with a Clear Intention**
   Set the tone for your day with a purposeful intention. For example: "Today, I'm focusing on noticing how biases might affect my decisions and interactions. My goal is to observe without judgment and reflect on what I can improve." By framing the day this way, you'll remain open, curious, and ready to learn from your experiences.

2. **Document Bias**
   Bring along a small notebook or use a digital tool like your phone's notes app to document moments where bias might have influenced your thinking or actions. Write down specifics about conversations, decisions, or situations that prompt you to reflect.

3. **Observe Key Moments**
    Throughout the day, pay close attention to your
    interactions, especially in meetings, one-on-one
    discussions, or decision-making scenarios. Use these
    guiding questions to prompt reflection:

    - Did I make assumptions based on someone's
      appearance, background, or role?

    - Did I favor a familiar perspective over a new
      or less familiar one?

    - Did I intentionally include diverse viewpoints
      in my decision-making process?

    Document your reactions honestly. The goal is to
    notice and understand, not judge.

4. **Look for Bias Triggers**
    After each key interaction, take a moment to think
    about what may have triggered any biases. Was it
    someone's experience level, communication style, or a
    shared background? Recognizing these triggers can help
    you understand where your biases originate, making
    it easier to address them moving forward.

5. **Identify Patterns**
    At the end of your day, set aside time to review your
    notes. Look for recurring themes or biases that appeared
    multiple times. For instance:

    - Did I consistently default to familiar voices
      during meetings?

    - When did I rely on appearance or job titles to
      guide my decisions?

     DAVID L ZIMMERMAN, MSC, CPC

Identifying patterns is the first step toward making meaningful changes.

6. **Create an Action Plan**
Using your insights, develop a plan to address the patterns you identified. Conscious Calibration can guide your approach by encouraging small, actionable steps. For example:

- If you noticed a bias toward familiar perspectives: Make a habit of asking quieter or less familiar team members for their input during meetings.

- If appearance or background influenced decisions: Use a checklist to ensure you're focusing on objective criteria, not initial impressions.

- For role-based biases: Reassess contributions based on skills and outcomes, rather than job titles or assumptions tied to roles.

By intentionally applying these steps, you'll begin to counter biases and foster a more inclusive environment.

7. **Seek Accountability**
Share your experience with a colleague or mentor you trust. Discuss the biases you noticed, your action plan, and ask for their perspective. A trusted partner can offer valuable feedback and help hold you accountable for staying on track.

8. **Follow Up Regularly**
A Bias Awareness Day is a great starting point, but real progress happens over time. Consider revisiting this exercise monthly or quarterly. Use it as a way to

check in with yourself and reflect on how your efforts are evolving.

If regular self-checks, reflection, and Conscious Calibration become a discipline, you will improve. Over time, this process will become second nature, helping you lead with greater awareness and inclusivity.

CHAPTER 7

LEADERSHIP CATALYSTS

"Without reflection, we go blindly on our way,
creating more unintended consequences."

—Margaret J. Wheatley

I WAS LEADING A national business team at Wells Fargo back in 2006, and we were at a critical juncture for merging two new business groups. We were facing tight deadlines and mounting pressure to deliver scheduled results, and I prided myself on being a leader who was approachable and receptive to input. But one day, during a candid one-on-one meeting, Rachel, one of my senior team members, dropped a truth bomb.

"You don't really listen, David," she said, her voice hesitant but firm.

Her comment landed like a gut punch. My initial reaction was defensiveness. Didn't she see how open I was to feedback? I wanted to argue, to justify myself, to dismiss her observation as wrong. Instead, I took a breath and asked, "Could you give me an example?"

She shifted awkwardly in her chair but seemed determined to make her point. "In our strategy meeting yesterday, you asked the team for our thoughts. But before anyone could finish, you jumped in with your own solutions. It felt like you were only asking us as a formality, like you'd already made up your mind."

I felt heat rising in my cheeks: a mix of embarrassment and grudging acknowledgment that she might be right. "Was it only yesterday, or have you noticed this other times?"

She hesitated again, then nodded. "It happens frequently."

Her words lingered between us. We had always shared strong mutual respect, so we sat comfortably in the silence of this uncomfortable moment. I leaned back in my chair, exhaling slowly and trying to process her feedback. I looked out the window and replayed a few scenes in my head. Maybe I am just going through the motions. Am I really this oblivious to my own behavior?

"I hadn't realized I was doing that," I admitted quietly, breaking the silence. "It's not intentional. But now I can see how it impacts you and the team. What do you suggest I do?"

Rachel relaxed slightly, encouraged by my openness. "Well, maybe you could pause a bit longer when you ask for input, you know . . .to really let us finish. And then ask some follow-up questions before offering your own solution. It would show you genuinely heard our ideas and value them."

I nodded. "I appreciate the courage it took to share this with me. It's uncomfortable," I said with an awkward-but-genuine smile, "but incredibly helpful. I'll commit to working on this, and I'd appreciate your feedback as I do."

"Of course." She smiled gently, patting me on the arm. "I'd be happy to help."

As I reflected on the conversation in the following days, I realized that she was right. I wasn't truly seeking feedback; I was listening without actually hearing. It wasn't easy to accept, but her observation was spot on. I needed to shift from just asking for feedback to genuinely embracing it, even when it made me uncomfortable. To this day, that essential exchange has stayed with me as a reminder that listening deeply, reflecting honestly, and continuously adapting is a crucial component of leadership. From that day forward, I kept striving to make space for genuine dialogue, using mindfulness disciplines to stay present and receptive. Ultimately, this strengthened trust and collaboration within my team and made me a better leader.

Feedback and reflection are more than tools for improvement—they're opportunities to grow in self-awareness and adaptability. They help leaders uncover blind spots, strengthen relationships, and refine their approaches. But feedback alone isn't enough; it needs to be paired with mindful reflection. Mindfulness helps leaders process feedback without defensiveness, turning challenging insights into actionable growth.

Stanford Psychologist Carol Dweck's calls this a "growth mindset." Her research shows that leaders who see feedback as a chance to learn rather than a critique to avoid become more resilient, self-aware, and forward-thinking.[89] They understand that mistakes and challenges are steppingstones to greater effectiveness. Let's explore how feedback, reflection, and

---

[89]   Dweck, C. S. (2006). *Mindset: The new psychology of success.* Random House.

mindfulness intersect to create a foundation for transformative leadership. When you embrace these practices, you not only grow as a leader but also foster a team culture rooted in trust, growth, and continuous improvement.

THE POWER OF FEEDBACK AND REFLECTION

Reflection and feedback are the secret recipe for great leadership; they help you see where you are, figure out where you're headed, and bring your team along for the ride. Leaders who make feedback and reflection part of their routine aren't just reacting to problems as they pop up, they're staying ahead of the game. When you take the time to hear from others, you're not just getting their perspective, you're building stronger relationships and growing into a more adaptable and effective leader.

Reflection is what makes feedback click. It's how you turn feedback into something actionable and meaningful. You're giving yourself space to think about the feedback you received and ponder why you made certain decisions, how they played out, and what you might do differently next time. It's not always easy—nobody loves admitting where they went wrong—but it's when the magic happens. Neuroscience tells us that reflection can actually rewire the brain, strengthening pathways that support cognitive flexibility and emotional control. Regular self-reflection helps leaders manage stress better, think more clearly, and adjust their strategies on the fly. Think of it like building mental muscles that make you more adaptable to change. Behavior researchers Richard J. Davidson and Sharon Begley explain that these reflective practices don't just prepare you to handle challenges, they make you better at it over time.[90] The more you reflect, the more resilient and

---

[90] Davidson, R. J., & Begley, S. (2012). *The emotional life of your brain: How its unique patterns affect the way you think, feel, and live—and how you can change them.* Hudson Street Press.

adaptable you become, both in how you lead and in how you respond to the unexpected.

Leaders who seek feedback and embrace reflection become more self-aware, handle challenges with more composure, and set a great example for their teams. Research backs this up: reflective leaders are more empathetic, adaptable, and better at creating environments where people feel safe to speak.[91] Toss mindfulness into the mix, and you've got a winning combination. Mindfulness means approaching feedback with curiosity instead of defensiveness. It helps you hit pause on those knee-jerk reactions and really absorb what has been said. Instead of seeing feedback as criticism, you start seeing it as a chance to improve. When leaders adopt this mindset, it's contagious. People pick up on the shift and start embracing personal growth and awareness, too. So, how can you tap into the power of feedback and reflection? It's simple: follow the three steps of the Feedback-Reflection-Action Cycle.

1. **Seek Feedback:** Don't sit around waiting for feedback to land in your lap—go after it! Ask people at all levels for their input, from your peers and mentors to your team members. Tools like 360-degree feedback or working with a professional coach can give you a clear picture of both your strengths and areas where you could improve. Studies show that leaders who actively seek feedback tend to build more trust and stronger connections with their teams.[92]

---

[91] Goleman, D. (2006). *Emotional intelligence: Why it can matter more than IQ* (10th ed.). Bantam Books.

[92] Ashford, S. J., & Tsui, A. S. (1991). Self-regulation for managerial effectiveness: The role of active feedback seeking. *Academy of Management Journal, 34*(2), 251–280. *https://doi.org/10.2307/256442*

2. **Reflect on Insights:** Once you've received feedback, take time to let it sink in. Whether you journal, meditate, or just sit quietly with your thoughts, reflection helps you connect the dots and turn feedback into something you can act upon. Look for patterns, challenge assumptions, and think about what you can learn.

3. **Take Action:** Reflection is only half the battle; you've got to put what you've learned into practice. Set clear goals for yourself based on the feedback. Maybe it's improving how you communicate or being more inclusive in your decision-making. Whatever it is, make it specific and measurable. And don't forget to check in with the people who gave you feedback—they can help you track your progress and hold you accountable.

This cycle keeps personal and professional growth intentional and focused. It also makes it easier to recover from setbacks because you're not just reacting, you're learning and adapting every step of the way. And here's the kicker: it's not just about you. When you create a culture where feedback is welcomed and valued, your whole team benefits. People feel safe to share their thoughts, knowing their input matters and won't be used against them. You can set the tone by modeling how to take feedback with gratitude and curiosity. Thank the people who give it to you, ask questions to understand their perspective, and show them you're acting on their suggestions.

Encourage your team to share feedback with each other too. When feedback flows in every direction, it stops being about hierarchy and becomes a shared tool for improvement. It helps break down barriers and address concerns and fears. People become more comfortable with vulnerability, and everyone becomes more productive and collaborative as a result. Research shows that teams with high psychological safety—where people feel comfortable expressing themselves—are more innovative and engaged.[93]

By weaving feedback, reflection, and mindfulness into your leadership, you're building a foundation for continuous growth—not just for yourself but for everyone on your team. It's about creating an environment where every voice matters, every idea gets a fair shot, and every challenge is an opportunity to get better.

MINDFUL ADAPTATION

Mindful Adaptation combines the practice of mindfulness with a structured approach to integrating feedback, giving leaders a thoughtful and intentional way to grow. It's not about rushing to fix things or treating feedback as a personal critique. Instead, it encourages leaders to see feedback as an invaluable tool for progress. Leaders who embrace Mindful Adaptation intentionally pause, reflect on their responses, and implement targeted adjustments that align with both their personal development and organizational objectives.[94]

The process starts with something deceptively simple: pausing. This pause allows leaders to break away from reactive tendencies and create the mental space to consider feedback objectively. It's during this pause that leaders can evaluate what they've heard, assess their emotional reactions, and think crit-

---

[93] Edmondson, A. C. (1999). Psychological safety and learning behavior in work teams. *Administrative Science Quarterly, 44*(2), 350–383. *https://doi.org/10.2307/2666999*

[94] Brown, K. W., & Ryan, R. M. (2003). The benefits of being present: Mindfulness and its role in psychological well-being. *Journal of Personality and Social Psychology, 84*(4), 822–848. *https://doi.org/10.1037/0022-3514.84.4.822*

ically about the implications. This gap between stimulus and response, what mindfulness expert Jon Kabat-Zinn describes as "non-reactivity," becomes the foundation for deliberate and constructive action.[95] By doing so, leaders shift from reacting out of habit or ego to responding in ways that are aligned with their goals and values.

What makes Mindful Adaptation particularly powerful is its impact on emotional regulation and decision-making. Research shows that leaders who regularly practice mindfulness experience improved emotional control, greater cognitive flexibility, and enhanced clarity in their choices. This means they're better equipped to handle high-pressure situations, interpret feedback without defensiveness, and approach challenges with creativity and composure.[96] For example, instead of dismissing feedback as criticism, a leader practicing Mindful Adaptation might recognize it as an opportunity to improve their approach or gain a fresh perspective.[96] But the benefits don't stop at the individual level. Leaders who practice Mindful Adaptation set a tone for their teams. When you consistently demonstrate openness to feedback, it sends a clear message to your team that growth and improvement are valued. This approach can cultivate a culture where everyone feels safe to share insights, explore new ideas, and embrace change. As a result, teams become more adaptive, collaborative, and cohesive.

By modeling this behavior, leaders inspire similar practices within their teams. This creates a ripple effect of mindfulness, openness, and reflection, which strengthens collective

---

[95]   Brown, K. W., & Ryan, R. M. (2003). The benefits of being present: Mindfulness and its role in psychological well-being. *Journal of Personality and Social Psychology, 84*(4), 822–848. *https://doi.org/10.1037/0022-3514.84.4.822*

[96]   Kabat-Zinn, J. (2003). Mindfulness-based stress reduction (MBSR). *Center for Mindfulness in Medicine, Health Care, and Society.*

adaptability and enhances team cohesion. Research further highlights that leaders who foster this kind of culture build resilience across their organizations, equipping teams to navigate uncertainty and change more effectively.[97]

Mindful Adaptation is not just a personal tool; it's a leadership philosophy. By grounding decisions in both feedback and reflection, leaders position themselves to thrive in complex, fast-changing environments. It equips them to maintain balance, stay aligned with organizational objectives, and continuously grow. Ultimately, this practice becomes a cornerstone of resilient leadership, empowering leaders to adapt thoughtfully and create lasting impact. Daniel Goleman points out that when leaders integrate mindfulness into their routines, they become more composed, empathetic, and resilient—all traits that contribute to a culture of reflection and continuous improvement.[98]

Embracing a Growth Mindset At the beginning of the chapter, I mentioned Dweck's concept of a growth mindset. It's a game-changer for leaders, so let's dive a little deeper. When you have a growth mindset, you believe that learning never stops and that setbacks are just steppingstones on your path of personal and professional growth. Leaders who adopt this mindset don't see challenges or mistakes as failures—they see them as opportunities to develop new skills, refine their strategies, and become stronger. Leaders with a growth mindset believe they can develop their skills and intelligence through

---

[97]　Brown, K. W., & Ryan, R. M. (2003). The benefits of being present: Mindfulness and its role in psychological well-being. *Journal of Personality and Social Psychology, 84*(4), 822–848. *https://doi.org/10.1037/0022-3514.84.4.822*

[98]　Goleman, D. (2006). *Emotional intelligence: Why it can matter more than IQ* (10th ed.). Bantam Books.

effort, learning, and persistence.[99] For them, feedback isn't something to fear—it's a tool for improvement. Setbacks? They're just part of the process. Leaders with this outlook show their teams that it's okay to take risks, make mistakes, and try again. This attitude creates a culture where innovation and engagement thrive, because people feel safe to experiment and grow. When leaders embrace feedback as a tool for growth rather than a critique of their worth, it sets the tone for everyone around them. Teams led by growth-minded leaders are more innovative and adaptable because they know mistakes are simply part of the learning process.[100]

KEY TAKEAWAYS

Together, feedback, reflection, mindfulness, and a growth mindset create a powerful framework for leadership. By staying open to learning from others, using reflection to strengthen adaptability, and practicing mindfulness to navigate challenges, leaders can build a foundation for high achievement and sustainable growth. This isn't just about improving leadership skills—it's about creating an environment where teams thrive, ideas flourish, and challenges are seen as opportunities to grow.

True leadership growth rarely happens in the heat of the moment. It is something that unfolds in the quiet space afterward—when feedback is examined, reflections are captured, and mindfulness turns insight into intentional action. Throughout this chapter we have seen that listening without judgment, pausing before reacting, and treating every comment as raw data for improvement are not peripheral "soft

---

[99] Dweck, C. S. (2006). *Mindset: The new psychology of success.* Random House.

[100] Dweck, C. S. (2006). *Mindset: The new psychology of success.* Random House.

skills," but core disciplines that separate reactive managers from adaptive leaders.

Begin by institutionalizing the Feedback-Reflection-Action Cycle. Seek perspective broadly—up, down, and laterally—because blind spots hide in familiar corners. Then carve out protected time to digest what you hear. Journaling, silent walks, or short meditative breaks will help to deepen your understanding from a safe, objective place, and prevent defensiveness from sabotaging this learning experience. Finally, convert reflection into one or two specific behavior changes you can test and measure. Small, visible wins reinforce credibility and encourage your team to engage in the same process.

Mindful Adaptation is the catalyst that keeps the cycle alive under pressure. The deliberate pause between stimulus and response creates room for choice: you can cling to ego or lean into growth. Neuroscience shows that each mindful pause strengthens neural pathways for empathy, focus, and cognitive flexibility. Over time, those moments compound into a leader who thrives in volatility rather than merely surviving it.

Lastly, adopting a growth mindset ties it all together. When mistakes become experiments and feedback becomes fuel, you model the psychological safety that sparks innovation. People speak up, iterate faster, and recover quickly because failure is reframed as tuition, not termination. Leadership transformation is not a leap but a loop: feedback informs reflection, mindfulness refines action, and action invites new feedback. Learn the loop and you will not only elevate your own effectiveness—you will ignite a culture where continuous improvement is the norm and extraordinary results are the inevitable byproduct.

- Feedback, reflection, and mindfulness are cornerstones of adaptive style of leadership. Together, they empower leaders to navigate challenges, enhance resilience, and drive personal and team growth.

- Mindful Adaptation transforms feedback into actionable insights. By combining mindfulness with reflection, leaders develop the self-awareness needed to respond to feedback thoughtfully and foster a culture of continuous improvement.

- A growth mindset and openness to feedback inspire team innovation and trust. Leaders who embrace feedback and prioritize self-awareness set a powerful example, building stronger, more cohesive teams and organizations.

CASE STUDY: REED HASTINGS'S COMMITMENT TO REFLECTION

Reed Hastings's journey at Netflix is a masterclass in using feedback and reflection to fuel growth and innovation. Since co-founding Netflix in 1997, Hastings has shown a remarkable ability to listen, adapt, and pivot—qualities that have transformed Netflix from a DVD rental company into the world's leading streaming platform. His story is a powerful example of how leaders can navigate challenges, make bold moves, and emerge stronger by staying open to feedback and reflecting deeply on their decisions.

When Netflix launched, Hastings and co-founder Marc Randolph reimagined the way people rented movies. Their subscription model allowed customers to rent DVDs by mail without worrying about late fees: a game-changing idea at the time.[101] Customers loved the convenience, and Netflix

---

[101]   Randolph, M. (2019). *That will never work: The birth of Netflix and the amazing life of an idea.* Little, Brown and Company.

   DAVID L ZIMMERMAN, MSC, CPC

quickly gained traction, but Hastings wasn't satisfied with just disrupting the DVD rental market. By the mid-2000s, he noticed a shift: broadband internet was becoming more accessible, and streaming video looked like the next big thing. Transitioning from physical DVDs to digital streaming was an ambitious move, requiring both technical innovation and significant investment. But Hastings's ability to reflect on industry trends and customer behaviors made him confident that this pivot was essential for Netflix's future.[102]

In 2011, Hastings made the bold but controversial decision to split Netflix into two brands: Netflix for streaming and Qwikster for DVD rentals. His goal was to position Netflix as a leader in streaming, but the move backfired. Customers were outraged by the added inconvenience and higher costs, and Netflix lost subscribers while its stock value plummeted by nearly 77%.[103]

Initially, Hastings defended the decision, but as customer frustration grew, he realized it was time to rethink the strategy. Instead of doubling down, Hastings stepped back to reflect on the feedback he was receiving from customers, employees, and analysts. He listened carefully to their concerns, acknowledged the mistakes, and decided to reverse the split. In an open letter to customers, he took full responsibility, admitting he had underestimated the impact of the changes and promising to do better.[104] This moment showcased Hastings's adaptive leadership. Rather than letting his ego get in the way, he used feedback to realign Netflix's strategy with customer needs. His

---

[102] Hastings, R., & Meyer, E. (2020). *No rules rules: Netflix and the culture of reinvention.* Penguin Press.

[103] Siklos, R. (2011, September 19). Netflix's self-inflicted wounds. *Fortune.* Retrieved from *https://fortune.com*

[104] Hastings, R., & Meyer, E. (2020). *No rules rules: Netflix and the culture of reinvention.* Penguin Press.

transparency and willingness to admit mistakes restored trust and strengthened Netflix's brand.

The Qwikster incident became a turning point for Hastings. It solidified his commitment to listening to feedback and using it to inform strategic decisions. Moving forward, Hastings doubled down on Netflix's streaming business and began investing heavily in original content like *House of Cards* and *Orange Is the New Black*. These bold moves paid off, setting Netflix apart from competitors and turning it into a global entertainment powerhouse.[105] Hastings also worked to create a culture of candor at Netflix. He encouraged employees to share honest feedback, challenge ideas, and contribute to decision-making processes. This culture of openness didn't just improve internal operations—it fueled innovation and resilience, allowing Netflix to stay ahead of industry trends and maintain its leadership in a rapidly evolving market.

Through his journey, Hastings demonstrated that feedback and reflection aren't just for course corrections—they're tools for long-term growth and innovation. His leadership shows how setbacks can become opportunities when approached with humility, openness, and a willingness to adapt. Reed Hastings's leadership story is a testament to the power of feedback, reflection, and adaptability in driving growth and innovation. By integrating these principles into your leadership, you can navigate challenges with resilience, inspire your team, and create lasting positive impact.

---

[105] Keating, G. (2018). *Netflixed: The epic battle for America's eyeballs.* Penguin Random House.

REFLECTION

Ask yourself the following questions and write your answers in your journal. After, take time to reflect on your discoveries.

1. Am I proactive about asking for feedback, and do I respond to it with curiosity rather than defensiveness?

2. What specific actions do I take to turn feedback into meaningful improvements in my leadership?

3. How do I use mindfulness to stay calm, process feedback constructively, and avoid reacting impulsively?

4. Does feedback from my team actively shape my decisions, and how can I make this connection more visible to them?

5. What steps am I taking to build a culture where feedback flows freely, and how do I model this openness for my team?

SELF-AUDIT

Rate yourself on a scale from one to ten, where one means "rarely or not at all" and ten means "frequently or very well."

1. I seek feedback from diverse sources to improve my leadership approach.

    1   2   3   4   5   6   7   8   9   10

2. I regularly set aside time to reflect on feedback and my leadership decisions.

    1   2   3   4   5   6   7   8   9   10

3. I practice mindfulness to stay present and open when receiving feedback.

    1   2   3   4   5   6   7   8   9   10

4. I translate feedback into actionable steps for my personal and professional growth.

1   2   3   4   5   6   7   8   9   10

5. I create an environment where my team feels safe to share honest feedback.

1   2   3   4   5   6   7   8   9   10

6. I approach setbacks and criticism as opportunities to learn and grow.

1   2   3   4   5   6   7   8   9   10

7. I actively demonstrate how I apply feedback to my decisions and leadership style.

1   2   3   4   5   6   7   8   9   10

8. I encourage open dialogue within my team, modeling how to give and receive feedback.

1   2   3   4   5   6   7   8   9   10

9. I use reflection and feedback to adjust my leadership strategies to meet evolving needs.

1   2   3   4   5   6   7   8   9   10

10. I commit to continuous learning by incorporating reflection, feedback, and mindfulness into my routine.

1   2   3   4   5   6   7   8   9   10

EXERCISE: WEEKLY REFLECTION PRACTICE

Set aside thirty minutes each week to reflect on recent decisions, feedback received, and how they align with your leadership goals. Write down specific actions you can take to integrate this feedback into your approach. Over time, assess how this practice influences your resilience and decision-making.

CHAPTER 8

THE POWER OF VULNERABILITY

*"Vulnerability is the birthplace of innovation,
creativity, and change."*

—Brené Brown

I T WAS A crisp autumn morning in 2008 at the height
of the 2008–2010 financial crisis, known as the Great
Recession, one of the most severe economic downturns since
the Great Depression. I vividly remember standing in front of
the television in my office at Wells Fargo Advisors in Beverly
Hills shaken to my core. Just hours earlier, news had broken
that Lehman Brothers had filed for bankruptcy. Having worked
there earlier in my career, it seemed unfathomable that this
titan of finance was now in a death spiral. Watching the news
unfold made me feel physically ill, given the impact this crisis
was having on even the biggest banks and financial institutions
across the country—forget the fact that I had a pension on

their balance sheet! An icy chill had spread through my chest as reality sunk in. This wasn't just another market hiccup—it was an earthquake rattling the very foundations of my industry.

Later that afternoon, the weight of the day would grow even heavier as I prepared to discuss a crisis closer to home. I entered the conference room, where everyone was somber. Even all the natural light flooding in through the room's floor-to-ceiling windows couldn't lighten the mood. My team was gathered around the large conference table looking worried and fatigued. Papers and half-filled coffee cups lay scattered everywhere, a testament to our desperate, sleepless efforts to save an acquisition that had gone south. We had spent months fighting to save this critical new business, only to see it collapse.

Facing this epic failure, I had my list of excuses ready. There were extreme market conditions, unforeseen corporate challenges, and countless external factors that made it easy to shift blame. But looking at the eleven emotionally depleted senior leaders who'd given it their all to try to fix things, I realized that excuses wouldn't help. What they needed wasn't a leader who could justify failure, but one who could take responsibility for it.

"This one's on me," I said. "I didn't anticipate many of the risks, and I should have asked more questions when we hit roadblocks. I let you down."

The room went silent, and I braced for their disappointment and frustration to be unleashed. Instead, something unexpected happened. Susan, our senior analyst, cleared her throat softly. Her eyes met mine, hesitant but sincere. "Honestly, David, it wasn't just you. I saw some of these red flags early on but didn't speak up because I thought we had it under control. I regret not raising my concerns sooner."

"I agree," James, our head of operations, had chimed in. "When we started seeing the cracks in the industry forming, I assumed the issues would resolve themselves. I should have been more proactive in bringing solutions rather than waiting."

Across the table, Rebecca, our compliance director, nodded thoughtfully as she spoke. "We've all been stretched thin and focused on putting out immediate fires. Maybe we overlooked strategic discussions. Moving forward, we need to prioritize those conversations more deliberately."

The dialogue continued, each person courageously owning their part in the project's collapse. With every open and heartfelt contribution, the tension dissipated more. It wasn't about pointing fingers, but about collective accountability. Finally, Mike, the lead project manager, spoke up decisively. "We've learned some hard lessons here. The market is unpredictable and beyond our control, that's for sure. But how we respond, how we communicate, that is something we *can* control. Let's agree to address risks more openly and earlier, even when it feels uncomfortable."

I felt intense gratitude and a renewed sense of resolve as I listened to each team member speak.

"I appreciate everyone's honesty," I said, feeling a great weight lifted off my chest. "These conversations are never easy, but they are necessary. Let's use this moment as a turning point. Moving forward, let's build a culture where it's safe and encouraged to speak up, no matter how tough the message."

Heads nodded around the table. It was a humbling but transformative moment. In our shared vulnerability, we began to rebuild trust and resilience, preparing to face whatever came next together. What could have been a demoralizing turned into a powerful conversation about how our team would work together going forward.

That day, I learned an important truth about leadership: vulnerability isn't about exposing weakness—it's about creating connection. By admitting my own shortcomings, I'd given my team permission to do the same. It was the beginning of a new way of doing things, a new team culture. We rebuilt trust, strengthened our resolve, and emerged as a more cohesive unit.

AUTHENTIC LEADERS ARE VULNERABLE

Vulnerability in leadership is often misunderstood. For decades, leaders were expected to project nothing but confidence, certainty, and complete control at all times. But the reality is, leadership isn't about having all the answers or getting it right every time. Mistakes happen. Effective leadership today involves creating an environment where people feel safe to explore, experiment, fail, learn, and grow. Vulnerability is the foundation. It's what allows leaders to admit mistakes, seek input, and show their humanity—all of which are essential for building trust and a strong resilient culture where authenticity and openness thrive. Think about it, when a leader admits they don't have all the answers or openly seeks input, they send a clear message to their team: "It's okay to be human here." That's the kind of authentic leadership that fosters trust.

When leaders choose to share their challenges, accept pitfalls and failures with humility, and remain genuinely open to feedback, they build a culture where transparency isn't just encouraged—it's the norm. This openness helps team members feel secure enough to share their own ideas, raise concerns, and take risks without fear of judgment. In turn, this builds what Professor Amy Edmondson of Harvard Business School calls "psychological safety," which is the belief that one will not be punished or humiliated for speaking up with ideas, questions, concerns, or mistakes.[106]

Bestselling Author Brené Brown hits the nail on the head when she refers to vulnerability as "the birthplace of innovation, creativity, and change."[107] And isn't that what great leadership is about? Leaders must *lead* the way, after all—meaning that wherever leaders go, others follow. By modeling vulnerability, leaders demonstrate that learning and growing together is more meaningful than perfection. When leaders admit to their mistakes and are consistently open to new perspectives, they lead the way to an environment in which everyone feels empowered to innovate, contribute, and collaborate.

This ties directly into other foundational concepts we've explored, like feedback and reflection. Vulnerability is what makes feedback more than a transaction, it makes it meaningful. When a leader says, "Here's where I'm struggling. What do you think?" or "I'm open to learning a better way," it not only invites dialogue but also shows that feedback is a two-way street. By modeling openness, leaders create an environment where innovation thrives, risks are rewarded, and shared accountability becomes a core value. This strengthens resilience and builds trust.

VULNERABILITY BUILDS TRUST

Yes, one of the most positive side effects of vulnerability is trust—the currency of achievement. When a culture of genuine trust exists, leaders and teams are able to navigate decisions

---

[106] Edmondson, A. C. (2018). *The fearless organization: Creating psychological safety in the workplace for learning, innovation, and growth*. Wiley.

[107] Brown, B. (2012). *Daring greatly: How the courage to be vulnerable transforms the way we live, love, parent, and lead*. Gotham Books.

and challenges together and reach their goals in a sustainable way. So, the next time you think about leadership, ask yourself: How am I showing vulnerability in a way that inspires trust and openness? Paul Zak, a professor of psychology and management at Claremont Graduate University, backs this up in his research, showing that teams that have a foundation built on trust communicate better, engage more deeply, and perform at higher levels.

Vulnerability, when tied to trust, can be the difference between a stagnant team and one that thrives.[108] Think of it this way: When leaders share how they navigated a difficult decision or rebounded from a mistake, they demystify the fear of failure. They're not just saying, "I've been there," they're showing that setbacks are a natural, and essential, part of growth. This openness encourages team members to step out of their comfort zones, take calculated risks, and bring their whole selves to work.

But here's the kicker—it's a two-way street. When leaders model vulnerability, it creates space for team members to share their own challenges and aspirations, paving the way for deeper collaboration and more innovative problem-solving. Imagine a leader saying, "I didn't handle this situation as well as I could have. Here's what I've learned . . ." and then following up with the question, "What are your thoughts?" This is bigger than vulnerability; it's leadership in action. And in leading by example, it demonstrates in real time how growth is a constant and vital part of everyday business, not just something you talk about twice a year at team-building retreats. It's actually a team core value! This is extremely powerful. It's about creating a team culture where people feel safe enough to say, "I need

---

[108] Zak, P. J. (2017). *Trust factor: The science of creating high-performance companies.* AMACOM.

help," or "I have an idea," because they know they'll be met with the support and respect they deserve. This, in turn, creates a cycle of continuous learning and improvement that benefits not just individuals but the entire organization. Ultimately, this approach is a reminder to us all that trust isn't automatic—it is something that is earned, nurtured, and strengthened over time through consistent, authentic leadership that includes vulnerability. And this is what empowers teams to collaborate freely, innovate boldly, and grow together in meaningful ways.

VULNERABILITY AND TEAM DYNAMICS

I hope it is becoming clear that when leaders embrace vulnerability, they unlock the door to deeper connections, better communication, and a stronger sense of trust within their teams. That's why it's such a game-changer for team dynamics. Again, it's not about oversharing; it's about showing that you're human, approachable, and open to learning. Here's how vulnerability creates a ripple effect:

Enhanced Communication

When leaders show vulnerability, they set the tone for honest and open communication. By creating an environment where people feel safe sharing ideas, concerns, and even mistakes, you're inviting a diversity of perspectives into the room. This openness is especially powerful in complex problem-solving. Teams that feel free to speak up are more likely to collaborate effectively and innovate. Vulnerability signals to your team that their voices matter, encouraging them to contribute without fear of being shut down.

Increased Engagement and Motivation

Think about how much more engaged you feel when you know your leader is relatable and authentic. Vulnerable leaders don't hide behind a façade of perfection; they admit when they don't have all the answers and value the contributions of their team. This creates genuine connections that motivate employees to go above and beyond. Author Brené Brown has shown that when leaders build real connections with their teams, employees feel valued and more inspired to bring their full selves to work.[109] That level of connection can transform a team from simply functioning to truly thriving.

Building Resilience Through Openness

Life throws curveball and so does work. Teams led by vulnerable leaders tend to be more resilient because they're taught to see challenges not as

---

[109] Brown, B. (2018). *Dare to lead: Brave work. Tough conversations. Whole hearts.* Random House.

failures but as opportunities to learn and grow. When leaders openly acknowledge their setbacks and model how to bounce back, they show their teams that it's okay to stumble; it's how you get back up that matters. This attitude strengthens the individual as much as it strengthens the team, building a culture that thrives under pressure. Vulnerable leaders turn challenges into collective growth moments.

Establishing Psychological Safety

One of the most powerful impacts of vulnerability is its ability to create psychological safety. Amy Edmondson's research makes it clear: teams perform at their best when they feel safe to take risks, voice concerns, and even make mistakes.[110] Vulnerable leaders set this tone by being transparent about their own missteps and engaging openly with their team. It's not just about admitting mistakes—it's about creating an environment where everyone feels comfortable learning from them. When your team knows they can take risks without fear of judgment, that's when innovation and creativity really take off.

Ultimately, vulnerability is about creating a workplace where people feel seen, heard, and respected. It's not about appearing weak; it's about showing strength through honesty and a willingness to grow. When leaders embrace vulnerability, they empower their teams to do the same, fostering an environment where communication flows freely, resilience is built into the

---

[110] Edmondson, A. C. (2018). *The fearless organization: Creating psychological safety in the workplace for learning, innovation, and growth*. Wiley.

culture, and everyone feels safe enough to take bold steps forward. And that is when the magic happens.

KEY TAKEAWAYS

For decades, conventional wisdom urged leaders to mask uncertainty and press on with unwavering confidence. Based on the research of others, and my extensive experience in leadership, I am arguing for the opposite: sustainable performance is born of courageous transparency.

When you admit what you don't know, invite people to disagree with you, and share where you've stumbled, something shifts. People stop performing and start contributing. They speak up earlier, challenge ideas before those ideas become expensive mistakes, and take risks without fearing career consequences. This isn't soft leadership—it's smart leadership. Saying "I got that wrong" or "I'm still figuring this out" replaces the fear of failure with a sense that we're all in it together. And that openness compounds over time. When people feel safe to experiment, they treat setbacks as lessons rather than embarrassments. They grow faster, innovate more, and stick around longer. If you want to make this real, build habits around it: debrief decisions openly, create space for honest conversation, and celebrate smart risks even when they don't pan out. Let people see your own growth edges, not just your expectations of theirs.

Leadership ultimately hinges on choices made in the face of uncertainty. The leaders who excel are those who harness vulnerability to gather richer intelligence, test hypotheses quickly, and adapt decisively. They convert personal humility into organizational strength. You can transform vulnerability from a private risk into a public asset—one that fortifies trust, sharpens judgment, and positions your organization to thrive amid constant change.

- Vulnerability is a cornerstone of effective leadership, fostering openness, strengthening relationships, and creating an environment of psychological safety.

- Practicing vulnerability as a leader builds resilience, both individually and within teams, by demonstrating how setbacks and challenges can lead to growth and learning.

- Leaders who align their actions with their values create trust through consistency and integrity, inspiring loyalty and fostering a cohesive, engaged team environment.

CASE STUDY: HOWARD SCHULTZ'S TRUST-BUILDING AT STARBUCKS

Howard Schultz's return to Starbucks in 2008 offers a masterclass in how vulnerability and trust-building can revitalize a struggling organization. At the time, Starbucks was reeling from declining profits, eroding customer loyalty, and a brand identity that had drifted away from its roots. Instead of dictating solutions from the top, Schultz adopted a transparent, collaborative approach that leaned heavily on vulnerability and trust to guide the turnaround.

One of Schultz's first actions was a bold public acknowledgment of Starbucks' challenges. He admitted that rapid expansion had caused the company to lose focus on what made it special: delivering exceptional coffee and memorable customer experiences.[111] In an unprecedented move, he shut down more than 7,000 stores for a day to retrain baristas on espresso-making techniques. While some saw this as a symbolic

---

[111] Schultz, H., & Gordon, J. (2011). *Onward: How Starbucks fought for its life without losing its soul.* Rodale Books

gesture, Schultz used it to signal a renewed commitment to quality and consistency.

More importantly, Schultz prioritized listening. Recognizing that trust is built through mutual respect and dialogue, he invited Starbucks' employees, whom he referred to as "partners," to share their honest feedback about the company's shortcomings and areas for improvement. Forums and meetings became spaces for genuine two-way communication, where employees could voice their concerns and ideas without fear of judgment.[112,113] This open dialogue not only deepened trust but also empowered employees to contribute meaningfully to Starbucks' reinvention.

Schultz understood that restoring trust required more than just words—it required consistent, value-driven action. One of his key priorities was enhancing employee benefits. He expanded healthcare coverage, increased stock ownership opportunities, and invested in professional development programs to ensure employees felt valued and cared for.[114] Schultz believed that when employees felt supported, they would deliver better service to customers, creating a virtuous cycle of trust and engagement.

Another cornerstone of Schultz's approach was Starbucks' commitment to social responsibility. Schultz reinvigorated the company's focus on ethically sourced coffee, strengthening relationships with coffee farmers and ensuring sustainable practices. At the same time, he spearheaded store redesigns to create welcoming, community-oriented spaces that fostered

---

[112] Schultz, H., & Gordon, J. (2011). *Onward: How Starbucks fought for its life without losing its soul.* Rodale Books

[113] Covey, S. M. R., & Merrill, R. R. (2006). *The speed of trust: The one thing that changes everything.* Free Press.

[114] Moon, Y., & Quelch, J. A. (2003). Starbucks: Delivering customer service. *Harvard Business School Case Study.*

connection and conversation. These efforts reinforced Starbucks' mission to be a "third place" for customers, bridging home and work with a sense of belonging.[115,116]

Schultz's leadership during Starbucks' turnaround was defined by a delicate balance of vulnerability and decisiveness. He openly acknowledged the company's struggles, took responsibility for past missteps, and modeled a willingness to learn and adapt. This vulnerability resonated deeply with employees and customers alike, creating a renewed sense of purpose and alignment with Starbucks' values.

At the same time, Schultz demonstrated steadfastness in his actions. He consistently aligned his decisions with the company's mission, whether by pausing expansion to refocus on quality, emphasizing sustainability, or investing in his team's well-being. These actions sent a clear message: Starbucks was committed to earning back trust, not through rhetoric but through meaningful, tangible changes.[117]

The results were striking. Starbucks regained customer loyalty, boosted employee morale, and returned to profitability. Schultz's ability to blend vulnerability, transparency, and decisive action turned Starbucks' challenges into a platform for transformation, proving that trust-building leadership is not only impactful, but essential for long-term success.

---

[115] Schultz, H., & Gordon, J. (2011). *Onward: How Starbucks fought for its life without losing its soul.* Rodale Books.

[116] Edmondson, A. C. (2018). *The fearless organization: Creating psychological safety in the workplace for learning, innovation, and growth.* Wiley.

[117] Gallo, C. (2014). *The Starbucks experience: 5 principles for turning ordinary into extraordinary.* McGraw Hill.

REFLECTION

Ask yourself the following questions and write your answers in your journal. After, take time to reflect on your discoveries.

1. How do you currently model vulnerability in your leadership, and how might doing so more intentionally build trust within your team?

2. Think of a recent challenge where you chose not to share your concerns with your team. What might have been the outcome if you had embraced vulnerability in that moment?

3. How do your actions align with your organization's core values, and how can demonstrating vulnerability strengthen that alignment?

4. In what ways can you create opportunities for open, two-way feedback to foster trust and encourage innovation within your team?

5. How do you ensure that your vulnerability builds trust without undermining your team's confidence in your leadership?

SELF-AUDIT

Rate yourself on a scale from one to ten, where one means "rarely or not at all" and ten means "frequently or very well."

1. I embrace vulnerability as a strength that promotes trust and connection within my team.

   1   2   3   4   5   6   7   8   9   10

2. I create an environment where team members feel safe to express themselves without fear of judgment.

1   2   3   4   5   6   7   8   9   10

3. I share my challenges and lessons learned to inspire growth and authenticity in my team.

1   2   3   4   5   6   7   8   9   10

4. I actively listen to my team's feedback and adjust my approach based on their insights.

1   2   3   4   5   6   7   8   9   10

5. I model psychological safety by being open about my mistakes and showing how I learn from them.

1   2   3   4   5   6   7   8   9   10

6. I balance vulnerability with decisiveness to maintain my team's confidence in my leadership.

1   2   3   4   5   6   7   8   9   10

7. I consistently align my leadership practices with the values I communicate to my team.

1   2   3   4   5   6   7   8   9   10

8. I encourage my team to share their ideas and challenges, cultivating a collaborative culture.

1   2   3   4   5   6   7   8   9   10

9. I actively seek opportunities to demonstrate trust-building vulnerability in my leadership.

1   2   3   4   5   6   7   8   9   10

10. I promote resilience within my team by emphasizing growth and learning through setbacks.

1   2   3   4   5   6   7   8   9   10

EXERCISE: PRACTICING LEADERSHIP VULNERABILITY

Here are six steps you can take to practice vulnerability and get comfortable with a more transparent approach to leadership. I encourage you to journal the experience.

1. **Choose a Personal Leadership Experience**
   Reflect on a significant leadership experience; this could be a moment of triumph, a challenge you overcame, or a mistake that provided valuable lessons. The experience should be meaningful and relevant to your current team dynamics or organizational goals.

2. **Frame the Story with Purpose**
   Prepare to share this experience with your team, focusing on the lessons you learned and how it shaped your leadership approach. Highlight how the experience aligns with your values and vision for the team.

3. **Encourage Team Participation**
   Invite team members to share their own experiences, framing the conversation as an opportunity for growth and connection. Use prompts like:

   - "What's a moment in your career where you learned something important through a challenge?"

   - "How has a personal mistake helped you grow professionally?"

4. **Facilitate an Open Discussion**
   Lead the discussion by modeling openness and curiosity. Acknowledge and appreciate the stories shared by team members, emphasizing that vulnerability and reflection are strengths that build trust and drive growth.

5. **Reflect and Plan for Growth**
    After the discussion, take time to reflect on its impact on team dynamics. Consider:

    - Did this exercise increase trust and engagement among team members?

    - Did anyone share ideas or concerns they hadn't expressed before?

    - How can this exercise inform your future approach to building psychological safety and fostering openness in the team?

6. **Follow Up with Consistency**
    Reinforce the value of vulnerability by integrating these discussions into regular team meetings or one-on-one check-ins. Celebrate moments of openness and demonstrate consistency by sharing updates on your own growth and learning as a leader.

CHAPTER 9

SOCIAL IDENTITY AND GROUP DYNAMICS

*"To be yourself in a world that is constantly
trying to make you something else is the greatest
accomplishment."*

—Ralph Waldo Emerson

WHILE AT RBC Dain Rauscher in the late 1990s, I
remember sitting in a boardroom with a team of senior
department directors, strategizing a path forward after a dismal
year. Tensions were high as everyone defended their turf while
budget cuts loomed. The marketing team wanted to preserve
their budget to protect the brand, operations was focused on
streamlining costs, and sales was pushing for aggressive expansion. Everyone was loyal to their respective groups, advocating
for solutions that aligned with their department's goals.

"We can't afford to cut back," insisted Laura, head of marketing, her voice firm. "Our brand reputation has already taken a hit."

Rob from operations shook his head as she spoke. "But costs are spiraling, Laura. We have inefficiencies everywhere; every dollar matters right now. If we don't streamline immediately, branding won't even matter because there won't be any resources left."

Brian from sales interrupted. "Streamlining sounds good on paper, Rob. But without aggressive growth, we'll just shrink our way into irrelevance. We need more resources focused on sales now, not less."

The arguments circled endlessly, department loyalties overshadowing organizational goals. No one openly attacked anyone else, but neither did they truly listen. We were stuck, trapped in our respective identities. Amid the cacophony of defensiveness and antagonism, I stood up slowly and signaled a pause.

"Okay, we're not getting anywhere. So, let's take a moment to remember why we're all here." I intentionally made eye contact with each department head as I spoke. "You are not just representing marketing, sales, or operations. Each of you is here as a leader in this firm. As such, it is your duty to unite around your commitment to serve our stakeholders and move this business forward. Understood?"

Heads nodded silently, and I let everyone sit in the quiet for a moment so they could recalibrate.

"Okay, good. Now, let's focus on what's best for the enterprise as a whole, rather than just our individual areas."

Laura was the first to speak again, her tone calmer this time. "Okay, perhaps we could be more targeted in our brand spending and prioritize what's critical until we get through this rough patch."

Rob leaned forward, visibly more relaxed. "Thank you, Laura. Maybe operations can identify which efficiencies actually enhance sales and marketing efforts as well as point out opportunities for expense reductions, rather than across-the-board cuts."

Brian jumped in with a rare concession. "Okay, if operations can free up some resources, my sales team could focus more on high-impact areas that drive growth without overstretching. I'm willing to roll up my sleeves, if you guys are."

The shift in energy was palpable. The team was back from the brink. Ideas began flowing in a more open and collaborative environment. By the end of the session, we'd outlined a plan that was cohesive, balanced, and most importantly, aligned with the organization's broader vision. It was a poignant reminder of how powerful it can be when leaders transcend their group identities to focus on their collective sense of purpose. The experience taught me that social identity is one of the most significant, yet often overlooked, forces in leadership. It shapes how we see ourselves, how we connect with others, and how we make decisions, especially at critical junctures. Understanding these dynamics is crucial, enabling us to bridge divides, foster unity, and create a culture where everyone feels they belong.

In this chapter, we'll explore the influence of social identity on leadership and decision-making. Drawing on the Social Identity Theory created by Polish Social Psychologist Henri Tajfel in 1978, we'll delve into how group dynamics impact team cohesion and performance. We'll also uncover strategies for leveraging social identity to create alignment, foster inclusivity, and lead with purpose—because great leadership isn't just about achieving results, it's about understanding the deeper forces that bring people together and using them to create something extraordinary.

*   *   *

SIDEBAR: HENRI TAJFEL'S SOCIAL IDENTITY THEORY

Why is Henri Tajfel's Social Identity Theory so important for leaders to understand? At its core, Tajfel's theory tells us something we all intuitively know. People draw a big part of their identity from groups. Whether it's a work team, a cultural organization, or even a shared hobby or sports group, these affiliations shape how we see ourselves and how we relate to others. Understanding this dynamic can help leaders build stronger, more cohesive teams. Tajfel's research on the "minimal group paradigm" revealed something fascinating: even under the simplest conditions, people show favoritism toward their own group and bias against others.[118] Think about how this might play out in the workplace. Team members naturally gravitate toward people they feel connected to, which can create a strong sense of loyalty and collaboration, but it can also spark competition or tension between different groups or cliques.

As a leader, your role is to harness the positive aspects of social identity while minimizing the potential downsides. For starters, understanding that people categorize themselves and others into groups helps you recognize the invisible forces at play in

---

[118] Tajfel, H., & Turner, J. C. (1979). An integrative theory of intergroup conflict. In W. G. Austin & S. Worchel (Eds.), *The social psychology of intergroup relations* (pp. 33–47). Brooks/Cole.

team dynamics. It's not just about who sits where or works on what project, it's about how people see themselves in the bigger picture and how that perception drives their behavior. Here's where Social Identity Theory becomes a practical tool for leadership. When you align team goals with your team members' sense of identity, you create a collective purpose that motivates everyone to pull in the same direction. Research backs this up; when people feel their personal identity aligns with the team's mission, they're more likely to be engaged, cooperative, and resilient.[119]

It's about making people feel that their contributions matter not just to the task at hand, but to the identity and success of the team as a whole. At the same time, understanding social identity can help you tackle common challenges, like internal competition or communication silos. By emphasizing shared goals and building a sense of solidarity, it is possible to help your team see their success as interconnected rather than competitive. This shift in perspective encourages collaboration and reduces conflict, creating an environment where people feel supported and valued.

Leaders who embrace this approach create an inclusive environment where diversity becomes a strength, not a division. Social Identity Theory shows us that when people feel their identity is respected and aligns with the organization's values, they're more likely to stay motivated, communicate openly, and contribute to the team's success.[120]

---

[119] van Knippenberg, D. (2000). Work motivation and performance: A social identity perspective. *Applied Psychology, 49*(3), 357–371. *https://doi.org/10.1111/1464-0597.00020*

[120] Ellemers, N., De Gilder, D., & Haslam, S. A. (2004). Motivating individuals and groups at work: A social identity perspective on leadership and group performance. *Academy of Management Review, 29*(3), 459–478. *https://doi.org/10.5465/amr.2004.13670967*

Imagine what your team could achieve if everyone felt that way. Leaders who get this right don't just build strong teams; they create communities where everyone feels connected to a common purpose—and that's when teams stop working together and start thriving together.

*   *   *

BALANCING PERSONAL IDENTITY IN GROUPS

Great leadership often comes down to one crucial balancing act: finding harmony between your personal identity and the collective identity of your team. It's not about losing yourself in the group or pushing your team to conform to your way of thinking—it's about blending these identities in a way that feels authentic and fosters real connection. When leaders openly share their values and beliefs while respecting the group's shared goals, it sends a powerful message: individuality and teamwork can coexist.

When you, as a leader, show up authentically, knowing and owning your values, you bring integrity to the table. This grounded perspective builds trust and creates a ripple effect throughout your team. Team members start feeling safer to bring their whole selves to work. This isn't just about creating a feel-good vibe; it's about building an environment where diverse perspectives thrive, leading to creative problem-solving and innovation. Social Identity Theory gives us some helpful context here. It explains that we get part of our self-worth from the groups we belong to, whether professional, cultural, sports, religious, or otherwise.[121] When leaders understand this, they can use it to strengthen team dynamics. It's not just

---

[121] Tajfel, H. (1978). *Differentiation between social groups: Studies in the social psychology of intergroup relations.* Academic Press.

about acknowledging someone's role or skills; it's about valuing what makes them unique while tying that uniqueness back to the group's broader mission. The payoff? Your team becomes more than just a collection of individuals. They start to see themselves as part of something bigger, something meaningful. This sense of alignment boosts morale and motivates everyone to work toward shared goals. Leaders who can strike this balance don't just improve team cohesion—they elevate the entire team's performance.

This is the art and science of Identity Dynamics, the weaving of personal and collective identities into a cohesive tapestry. When leaders respect and celebrate the unique perspectives and strengths of their team members, they create a culture where people feel truly valued. This isn't just a nice-to-have—it's essential for engagement and creativity. Research backs this up. Studies show that when leaders acknowledge individual identities while aligning them with the team's mission, they unlock higher levels of trust, innovation, and problem-solving.[122] The key to Identity Dynamics is balance. It's about making sure that individuality doesn't overshadow the team's collective purpose and that team goals don't stifle personal expression. Leaders who get this right create an environment where everyone can bring their full selves to work while feeling deeply connected to the team's shared vision. This kind of harmony builds a sense of belonging and accountability, making people more invested in the group's success. Imagine the impact this could have on your team. When people feel seen and appreciated for who they are, they're more motivated, engaged, and ready to contribute their best ideas—and when those individual efforts are guided toward a common goal, the

---

[122] Ashforth, B. E., & Mael, F. (1989). Social identity theory and the organization. *Academy of Management Review, 14*(1), 20–39. *https://doi.org/10.5465/amr.1989.4278999*

results can be transformative. So, how can you tap into Identity Dynamics as a leader? Start by showing genuine interest in the unique backgrounds and perspectives of your team members. Then, find ways to connect their personal strengths to the team's objectives. It's not just about getting people to work together—it's about creating a space where individuality fuels collaboration and drives collective success. That's the true power of Identity Dynamics.

KEY TAKEAWAYS

Social identity operates silently but powerfully in every group decision and juncture. Effective leadership begins with recognizing, not denying, the pull between individual social identity and group identity. On a practical level, this means stepping into every meeting willing to work on balancing both. When people trust that their individual perspectives will be heard and respected in a group, they are more willing to stretch beyond their typical comfort zone. This encourages more rigorous debate, balanced risktaking, and quality decision-making. Be willing to discuss your own values, invite others to share theirs, and visibly link those diverse viewpoints to the enterprise mission. Over time, the team will internalize a powerful new story: our differences expand our capabilities as a group in pursuit of common goals. That is the recipe for sustained high performance as a team.

- Social identity shapes leadership and team dynamics. Understanding this as a leader strengthens your ability to foster collaboration, mutual respect, and psychological safety. This creates a strong foundation for cohesive teamwork.

- Balancing individuality with collective purpose drives success. Leaders who align personal and group identities foster a shared sense of purpose while valuing individual contributions. This enhances creativity, inclusivity, and team unity.

- Inclusive leadership elevates engagement and performance. Leaders who prioritize inclusivity and actively harmonize diverse perspectives within their teams build trust, drive innovation, and create an environment where everyone feels empowered to contribute their best.

CASE STUDY: INDRA NOOYI FOSTERS AN INCLUSIVE CULTURE AT PEPSICO

Take a closer look at Indra Nooyi's remarkable leadership at PepsiCo and how she transformed the company into a model for inclusion and collaboration. During her time as CEO, Nooyi made it her mission to create a culture where everyone felt valued and empowered to contribute. Her approach to diversity and inclusion wasn't just about checking boxes, it was about building a workplace that celebrated individuality and encouraged people to bring their authentic selves to work every day. Nooyi understood something fundamental: when people feel like they belong, they perform at their best. To make this happen, she embedded inclusion into the core of PepsiCo's values. Under her leadership, the company launched programs aimed at increasing representation across all levels, from entry-level roles to the executive suite. But she didn't stop at hiring. Nooyi focused on creating an environment where diverse perspectives weren't just welcomed but were actively sought out and valued.[123]

---

[123] Bryant, A. (2014). Corner office: Indra Nooyi on being the only woman in the room. *The New York Times*. Retrieved from *https://www.nytimes.com*

One of her most impactful strategies was hosting regular town halls and listening sessions—not as formalities, but as an opportunity for employees to speak directly to the leadership team. Nooyi believed in the power of open communication and transparency, and she made sure every employee knew their voice mattered. This wasn't just about hearing people out; it was about showing respect and making employees feel like they were integral to the company's success.[124] Another game-changer was her "Performance with Purpose" initiative. This wasn't just a catchy slogan; it was a strategy that tied PepsiCo's business goals to social and environmental impact. Nooyi knew that employees wanted to work for a company that aligned with their values, so she focused on making PepsiCo a place where doing good went hand in hand with doing well. By aligning the company's mission with broader societal goals, Nooyi gave employees an even greater sense of purpose and motivation.[125]

Nooyi's unique approach to leadership wasn't just beneficial to internal culture, it extended to how PepsiCo served its customers and communities. She recognized that diversity didn't stop at the company's walls. To meet the needs of a global market, she invested in research and development to create products that reflected the tastes and preferences of diverse consumer groups. This move didn't just strengthen PepsiCo's market position, it also showed employees that their work was part of something bigger, something inclusive.[126]

---

[124]　PepsiCo. (2021). Diversity, equity & inclusion at PepsiCo. Retrieved from *https://www.pepsico.com*

[125]　Nooyi, I. (2018). *My life in full: Work, family, and our future.* Portfolio.

[126]　PepsiCo. (2021). Diversity, equity & inclusion at PepsiCo. Retrieved from *https://www.pepsico.com*

What really set Nooyi apart was her ability to balance visionary leadership with practical action. She didn't just talk about inclusion—she lived it through her policies and initiatives. By improving benefits, prioritizing sustainability, and focusing on creating a culture of openness, she demonstrated that inclusion isn't just good for morale, it's good for business. Employees became more engaged, customers felt understood, and PepsiCo thrived. Nooyi's story is a masterclass in how leaders can foster an inclusive culture that drives innovation and growth. She showed that when leaders prioritize diversity, listen to their teams, and align actions with their values, they create an environment where everyone feels they belong and can succeed. It's not just about being a good leader; it's about being the kind of leader who brings out the best in a company and its people.

REFLECTION

Ask yourself the following questions and write your answers in your journal. After, take time to reflect on your discoveries.

1. How do my personal values and experiences shape the way I lead and interact with my team?

2. What steps am I taking to actively recognize and respect the unique identities and backgrounds of my team members?

3. How do I balance fostering a collective team identity while encouraging individual contributions and perspectives?

4. In what ways can I create a culture where diversity is celebrated as a strength and team members feel empowered to bring their authentic selves to work?

5. How can I align the team's shared goals with the personal motivations and identities of its members to enhance collaboration and engagement?

SELF-AUDIT

Rate yourself on a scale from one to ten, where one means "rarely or not at all" and ten means "frequently or very well."

1. I reflect on how my personal identity shapes my leadership style and decisions.

   1   2   3   4   5   6   7   8   9   10

2. I encourage and create opportunities for team members to express their authentic selves.

   1   2   3   4   5   6   7   8   9   10

3. I actively seek to integrate diverse perspectives into team decision-making.

   1   2   3   4   5   6   7   8   9   10

4. I consistently align my leadership actions with the shared goals and values of the team.

   1   2   3   4   5   6   7   8   9   10

5. I demonstrate respect for the unique identities and cultural backgrounds of my team members.

   1   2   3   4   5   6   7   8   9   10

6. I create an environment where all individual contributions are acknowledged and valued.

   1   2   3   4   5   6   7   8   9   10

7. I model inclusive leadership behaviors that promote respect and collaboration.

   1   2   3   4   5   6   7   8   9   10

8. I proactively identify and address biases that may hinder team cohesion.

1   2   3   4   5   6   7   8   9   10

9. I foster open communication that bridges personal and collective team identities.

1   2   3   4   5   6   7   8   9   10

10. I work to build a shared team identity while celebrating individual uniqueness.

1   2   3   4   5   6   7   8   9   10

EXERCISE: CREATE A TEAM IDENTITY MISSION STATEMENT

This exercise is designed to harmonize individual identities with the team's collective purpose, fostering alignment and inclusivity.

1. **Start with Self-Reflection**
   Begin by having each team member reflect individually on their personal values, strengths, and what they feel they uniquely contribute to the team. Encourage them to think about how their identity shapes their approach to work and collaboration.

2. **Facilitate a Team Discussion**
   Bring the team together to share their reflections. Use prompts like:

   o   What values are most important to you, and how do they align with the team's purpose?

   o   How does your personal identity influence the way you approach team dynamics?

- This open dialogue encourages understanding and respect for individual identities.

3. **Identify Shared Values**
   Collaboratively identify the core values that resonate across the team. Discuss how these values contribute to the team's goals and how they can be integrated into everyday decision-making and interactions.

4. **Draft a Team Identity Statement**
   As a group, create a "Team Identity Statement" that reflects both the individuality of team members and the collective purpose of the team. This statement should emphasize inclusivity, respect, and shared commitment to the team's mission. For example: "We are a team that values individuality, respects diverse perspectives, and works together with integrity and purpose to achieve our shared goals."

5. **Apply the Statement in Practice**
   Identify specific ways the team can use this identity statement to guide decision-making, resolve conflicts, and build cohesion. For instance:

   - How can the statement serve as a reminder during challenging conversations?

   - How can it be incorporated into team rituals or meetings to reinforce unity?

6. **Reflect and Revisit**
   Revisit the Team Identity Statement periodically to ensure it remains relevant and reflective of the team's evolving dynamics. Use it as a touchstone for evaluating how well the team is balancing individual and collective goals.

CHAPTER 10

THE JUNCTURE CODE

"It is not the strongest or most intelligent who will survive but those who can best manage change."

—Charles Darwin

BEGINNING IN 2015, during my time as CEO of First Citizens Bank's broker-dealer, I encountered one of the most complex crossroads of my career. We were tasked with installing a new money management platform while simultaneously merging our business with a previously acquired firm's money management operation. Our team in FCIS was given priority to ensure our project's success but faced a hard deadline to free up resources for the trust department to address its ongoing issues. The stakes couldn't have been higher. Our team leaders were already stretched with their day-to-day responsibilities, and we were under-resourced to tackle a project of this magnitude. Expectations were immense, timelines were unforgiving, and the team was looking to me for direction. With so much to juggle, meetings were often unfocused.

One day, we'd prioritize client impact, and the next, advisor needs—all while trying to avoid any financial setbacks. By the end of each meeting, I was buried in spreadsheets, conflicting opinions, and mounting pressure to deliver results.

What stood out most during this time was my team's growing confusion. Without a structured approach to decision making, every proposed path seemed as uncertain as the last. I began to second-guess myself. Was I focusing on the right objectives or simply reacting to the loudest concern? After one particularly chaotic meeting, a junior team member approached me and said, "I think we're trying to solve ten problems at once. What if we started by figuring out what matters most?" It was a simple yet profound observation, and they were absolutely right.

That afternoon, the team and I sat down and sketched out a roadmap to bring order to the chaos. First, we identified our top priorities. Next, we analyzed risks and opportunities to refine our focus. Finally, we committed to a clear plan, established a rhythm for our daily communications, tracked our progress meticulously, and remained agile in making adjustments along the way. When we introduced this new approach to the team the next day, everything shifted.

Suddenly, we weren't just reacting—we were attacking problems with clarity and purpose. The roadmap gave us a shared language, a common understanding, and a sense of confidence that we could navigate the challenges together. Over the next several months, we didn't just meet our deadlines—we finished ahead of schedule and without major issues. The project became a defining moment for our team. It not only built trust and encouraged collaboration; it also gave us the confidence to tackle the remaining priorities and roadblocks on our transformational journey. Looking back, I realize this experience wasn't just about completing a challenging project; it was about learning how to lead with intention through uncertain times and situations. It was about discovering the power of a clear, repeatable process to guide decisions, unify my team, while building organizational resilience and focus.

FRAMEWORKS HELP LEADERS NAVIGATE UNCERTAINTY

As humans, we are wired by evolution to resist change. If the current moment is safe and secure, why change things and muck it all up? This is the thinking that kept us alive in our early days as a species. And it's one reason why change often feels uncomfortable, chaotic, and overwhelming. It's also why it's not easy for leaders to get a group of people to initiate or adopt change. Yet, in today's fast-paced business world, change is constant for leaders, teams, organizations, and industries. Leaders are asked to shepherd their people through a never-ending stream of adjustments while keeping everyone aligned through all the twists and turns. It's a lot of responsibility that almost never comes with a handbook or training. That's when having a structured process—a framework—becomes invaluable. The framework provides clarity amid the chaos and helps leaders stay focused on the bigger picture and true to their values while juggling competing priorities and perspectives.

Without a framework, it's easy to fall into reactive decision-making and lose focus on the ultimate strategic goal. Leaders often go into survival mode as emotions run high, information floods in, and the pressure to act feels paralyzing. A step-by-step approach offers stability. It doesn't eliminate every obstacle and challenge, but it does offer a clear, intentional path forward.

Dr. John Kotter, the Konosuke Matsushita Professor of Leadership Emeritus at the Harvard Business School, author, and founder of Kotter International, a management consulting firm based in Seattle and Boston, emphasizes that structured approaches to change help leaders organize new information, evaluate risks, and make decisions that align with their organization's long-term goals.[127] Frameworks don't just reduce stress and confusion, they ensure decisions are intentional and aligned with the broader mission at hand. This has powerful benefits, giving leaders an effective toolkit to evaluate options and priorities, weigh perspectives, and act with clarity and purpose. This inspires self-confidence. When leaders create a consistent and effective decision-making process, not only can they act with more confidence in the moment, but they inspire trust, the foundation of all strong relationships.

Over time, the currency of trust creates a strong foundation for ongoing, sustainable success. This is how high-performance teams not only survive, but thrive. When your team understands the principle's guiding decisions, it fortifies both alignment and cohesion. Expectations become clear and measurable, collaboration becomes more seamless, and everyone feels a sense of ownership. Research by Deborah Ancona, the Seley Distinguished Professor of Management as well as Professor of Organization Studies at MIT, shows that when teams align through structured decision-making frameworks, morale and productivity increase.[128] It's not just about knowing

---

[127]   Kotter, J. P. (1996). *Leading change*. Harvard Business Review Press.

[128]   Ancona, D., Malone, T. W., Orlikowski, W. J., & Senge, P. M. (2011). In praise of the incomplete leader. *Harvard Business Review.*

the *what*—it's also about understanding the *why* and *how*, which is what builds trust and accountability across the board.

Even with a framework, not every decision is going to be perfect. Sometimes time constraints compel you to decide without all the information you need. Sometimes circumstances change without warning. That's just the way business works in today's competitive environment. You can't let perfection prevent progress. You must take informed risks and that means sometimes you're going to get it wrong. What matters is how you learn from those moments. Part of any effective decision-making framework involves outcome assessment. This is how leaders and their teams figure out what has worked, what hasn't, and why. This powerful feedback loop is key. This cycle of reflection and improvement strengthens decision-making and will, over time, build an organization culture of growth and resilience. Peter Senge's work on learning organizations highlights this exact point. Organizations that embed learning into their processes, Senge says, are better equipped to adapt and thrive in a constantly changing world.[129]

THE JUNCTURE CODE

As a result of the stressful experiences of my early years as a leader, as well as the growing body of research supporting the game-changing power of decision-making frameworks, I developed the Juncture Code. What's the difference between a framework and a code? Frameworks establish the overarching direction and expectations for leaders, while codes provide the specific guidelines, steps, and behavioral standards that enable leaders to embody those expectations and drive positive outcomes for themselves and their teams. Think of a frame-

---

[129] Senge, P. M. (2006). *The fifth discipline: The art & practice of the learning organization.* Crown Business.

work as a house blueprint and a code as the structure for the rooms, bricks and mortar, electrical wiring, and the plumbing used to build the house step-by-step based on that blueprint. With a framework and supporting code, leaders ensure that everyone functions in alignment with intention, purpose, and integrity. Not only will the highly effective combo help you make more efficient decisions in the moment and keep you aligned with your mission amid the chaos of change, over time it will make you a better leader. By reducing the mental clutter and emotional overload that often come with the high-stakes decisions and challenges of change, it will help you stay focused and intentional. This creates a ripple effect; *your* clarity becomes *your team's* clarity, and together, you learn to navigate fluctuations and difficulties confidently and consistently.

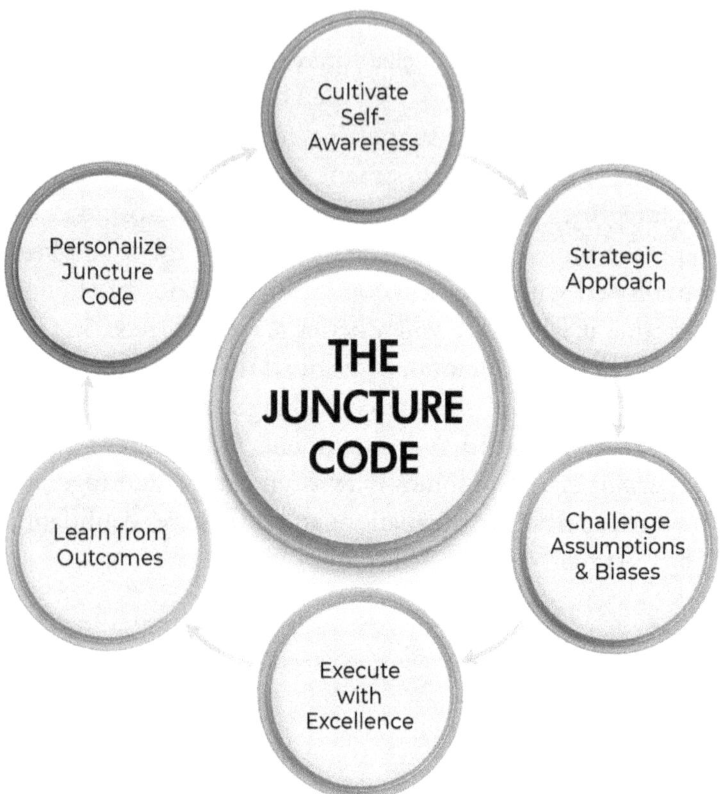

At its heart, the Juncture Code offers an agile structure to navigate business when things get complicated and decisions must be made. It will help you see opportunities where others see obstacles. You'll be able to guide your team with purpose and turn change into a catalyst for growth. You'll have a roadmap with clear steps to move forward, not just reactively, but with deliberate, mission-driven focus that empowers your teams to grow beyond their limits. Isn't that the essence of leadership? Whether you're leading a team through a crisis, managing a strategic pivot, or simply deciding what's next, the Juncture Code gives you the tools you need to move forward with clarity

     DAVID L ZIMMERMAN, MSC, CPC

and confidence. Here are the five steps of code, which we'll break down and explore in more detail in six separate chapters:

1. **Cultivate Self-Awareness:** Begin by deeply understanding yourself, your core values, biases, and motivations so you can approach decisions with integrity and authenticity.

2. **Take a Strategic Approach:** Analyze the data, situational factors, available resources, and potential outcomes; then, plan accordingly.

3. **Challenge Assumptions and Biases:** Question preconceived notions and habitual thinking. This can ignite fresh thinking and inspire teams to push beyond boundaries and drive meaningful innovation.

4. **Execute with Excellence:** Decide with clarity and intention and learn to balance short-term needs with long-term goals.

5. **Learn from Outcomes:** Reflect on your results to identify lessons and areas for growth.

6. **Personalize the Juncture Code:** This is when we explore making the code uniquely yours and customizing each of the steps, so they align with your personal values, experiences, and leadership vision.

KEY TAKEAWAYS

Change will always test leaders. My professional experience has taught me that when the stakes are high, the difference between confusion and progress lies in having a clear, intentional process. The Juncture Code emerged from those lessons; not as a rigid formula, but as a flexible, repeatable guide to navigate uncertainty with clarity and purpose. By combining self-awareness, strategic approach, curiosity, creativity, decisive action, and reflective learning, leaders can shift from reacting to circumstances to shaping them.

Frameworks bring order; codes bring action. Together, they provide a foundation strong enough to weather disruption and agile enough to seize opportunities. This balance of structure and adaptability allows leaders to make informed decisions without losing sight of values or vision. It also builds the trust, cohesion, and shared purpose that high-performing teams need to thrive in the midst of change. Yet the true power of the Juncture Code lies in personalization. When leaders align its steps with their own values, experiences, and goals, the process becomes a living extension of who they are—the framework governs, while the code must be lived. It grows and adapts as they do, creating a leadership style that is both effective and authentic. In a world where change is constant, your ability to lead with intention will define your success. The Juncture Code offers a roadmap to guide your team with clarity, confidence, and purpose.

- Structured Frameworks Enhance Decision-Making: A clear framework, supported by the Juncture Code, helps leaders manage complexity, ensuring decisions align with both immediate needs and long-term goals.

- Reflection Drives Leadership Growth: Integrating reflection into decision-making fosters a cycle of continuous learning, enabling leaders to adapt strategies and refine approaches over time.

- Adaptability Through Intentional Processes: By combining structure with flexibility, leaders can navigate change with confidence, maintaining focus on their vision while staying responsive to evolving circumstances.

CASE STUDY: AMAZON'S ITERATIVE MODEL OF CONSTANT IMPROVEMENT

Amazon's transformation from a small online bookstore into a global powerhouse in e-commerce, cloud computing, and technology is nothing short of remarkable. At the heart of this journey lies a relentless commitment to constant improvement and innovation as well as an approach that closely mirrors the principles of the Juncture Code. Jeff Bezos, founder and longtime CEO of Amazon, led with a clear focus on long-term thinking, data-driven decisions, and a willingness to challenge the status quo.

From the beginning, Amazon's culture was rooted in two key ideas: customer obsession and continuous innovations. This laser focus created a company ethos where every major step, whether expanding into new markets or launching innovative products, was carefully calculated. Amazon's approach has never been about chasing random opportunities. Instead, their decision-making framework empowers their leadership and people to take calculated risks while staying true to Amazon's mission.

One of the company's most iconic successes is Amazon Prime. What began as a simple idea—offering free two-day shipping for an annual fee—evolved into a sprawling membership platform that includes streaming, exclusive deals, and other perks. This transformation didn't happen overnight. When Bezos and his team first conceived of Prime, it was a leap of faith based on data showing that customers valued faster shipping. But instead of rolling out a massive, untested program, they started small, analyzed customer behavior, and continuously tweaked the service to make it more appealing. The iterative process was key. By testing new ideas with smaller groups, learning from outcomes, and refining their approach, Amazon turned Prime into a loyalty-driving engine. Today, Prime has millions of members worldwide and contributes significantly to Amazon's bottom line. It's a shining example of how structured experimentation and adaptation within a solid framework can deliver long-term results.[130]

Another groundbreaking success came from an unexpected source: cloud computing. What began as a way to improve Amazon's own internal computing capabilities turned into one of its most profitable ventures: Amazon Web Services (AWS). Initially, the idea of Amazon entering the cloud services market might have seemed far-fetched—they were known as a retailer, after all—but Bezos encouraged his team to challenge that assumption. Starting small, AWS launched as an experiment. By closely analyzing early results, listening to client feedback, and iterating on their offerings, AWS grew into a global leader in cloud computing. This ability to experiment, gather insights, and refine strategies is a hallmark of Amazon's iterative approach and speaks directly to the power of frameworks and the approach of the Juncture Code.[131]

One of Bezos's most enduring leadership principles is Amazon's "Day 1" philosophy. The idea is simple but profound: treat every day like the first day of the company, with the same energy, openness, and hunger to innovate. This mindset

---

[130] OpenExO. (2024, October 31). *Case Study—Amazon*. In *Exponential organizations 2.0* (Case 1103). OpenExO. *https://www. openexo.com/book/1103-case-study-amazon*

[131] Colvin, G. (2022, December 8). *How Amazon grew an awkward side project into AWS, a $60 billion behemoth. Fortune. https://www.fortune.com/longform/amazon-web-services-ceo-adam-selipsky-cloud-computing/*

promotes a culture of continuous learning and improvement—values that are embedded within the Juncture Code. Failures are seen as opportunities to grow. Bezos frequently reminded his teams that big innovations require risk, and risk sometimes results in mistakes. The key is to learn quickly and use each lesson to improve. This philosophy has helped Amazon stay agile and responsive, allowing it to tackle new challenges and enter new markets without losing sight of its core mission.

Jeff Bezos's leadership at Amazon demonstrates how a structured, adaptable approach to decision-making can fuel innovation, resilience, and long-term success. His focus on iterative improvement, data-driven decisions, and embracing risk offers a wealth of lessons for leaders seeking to navigate complexity and foster sustained growth.

REFLECTION

Ask yourself the following questions and write your answers in your journal. After, take time to reflect on your discoveries.

1. How effectively do I use structured frameworks like the Juncture Code to navigate pivotal decisions?

2. In what ways can I better align my decision-making processes with both short-term priorities and long-term organizational goals?

3. How do I currently incorporate iterative reflection and learning into my leadership practices, and where could I improve?

4. What challenges in my leadership might benefit from applying a more systematic and intentional framework?

5. How can I encourage my team to embrace a framework-driven approach to decision-making, fostering resilience and adaptability?

SELF-AUDIT

Rate yourself on a scale from one to ten, where one means "rarely or not at all" and ten means "frequently or very well."

1. I use a structured approach like the Juncture Code to guide my decision-making.

1	2	3	4	5	6	7	8	9	10

2. I consistently evaluate potential outcomes and their alignment with organizational goals before making decisions.

1	2	3	4	5	6	7	8	9	10

3. I challenge assumptions and seek diverse perspectives to refine my choices.

1	2	3	4	5	6	7	8	9	10

4. I develop and analyze multiple options before committing to a course of action.

1	2	3	4	5	6	7	8	9	10

5. I align my decision-making process with both immediate objectives and long-term vision.

1	2	3	4	5	6	7	8	9	10

6. I regularly reflect on past decisions to identify lessons and opportunities for improvement.

1	2	3	4	5	6	7	8	9	10

7. I adapt flexibly within a structured framework to handle changing circumstances.

1	2	3	4	5	6	7	8	9	10

8. I encourage my team to adopt a systematic approach to decision-making and problem-solving.

   1   2   3   4   5   6   7   8   9   10

9. I foster a culture of continuous reflection and learning within my organization.

   1   2   3   4   5   6   7   8   9   10

10. I feel confident and prepared to navigate critical junctures with clarity and purpose.

   1   2   3   4   5   6   7   8   9   10

EXERCISE: EXPLORE YOUR LEADERSHIP JUNCTURES

This exercise helps you start reflecting on the critical decisions you face in leadership and how a structured framework, like the Juncture Code, can begin to shape your approach.

Step 1: **Identify a Recent Leadership Crossroad.** Think about a specific moment in your leadership journey where you had to make a significant decision. Consider situations such as:

- Adapting to sudden changes.

- Balancing competing priorities.

- Addressing challenges in alignment with personal and organizational values.

Describe this crossroad in a few sentences, noting what made it pivotal or challenging.

Step 2: **Reflect on Your Process.** Ask yourself:

- How did I approach this decision?

- Did I have a clear process or framework to guide me?

- What challenges did I face in reaching a decision?

- Were my personal values or organizational goals part of the decision-making process?

Now, write a brief reflection on what worked well and what could have been improved in your approach.

Step 3: **Imagine Applying a Framework.** Consider how having a structured framework, such as the Juncture Code, could have impacted your decisions:

- Would it have provided more clarity or reduced uncertainty?

- How might it have helped you balance personal and organizational priorities?

- Could it have made you feel more confident in your decision?

Write down your thoughts on how using a repeatable process for decision-making could influence your leadership in similar situations.

Step 4: **Plan for the Next Juncture.** Looking ahead, identify an upcoming leadership challenge or decision point.

- How could you approach this situation differently using a structured framework?

- What aspects of the Juncture Code (such as intentionality, clarity, or adaptability) feel most applicable to this upcoming crossroad?

Write a few actionable steps you could take to prepare for this decision using what you've learned so far.

CHAPTER 11

BEGIN WITH SELF-AWARENESS

"Knowing yourself is the beginning of all wisdom."

—Aristotle

L ET'S START WITH a simple truth: You can't lead others effectively if you don't understand yourself. Self-awareness is the cornerstone of strong leadership, and for good reason. It's not just about knowing your strengths and weaknesses; it's about understanding how your personal values, motivations, and even your biases and blind spots influence the way you assess situations and act. When leaders are *truly* self-aware, their decisions become more intentional, and they create a sense of stability, trustworthiness, and authenticity that radiates throughout their teams and organizations.

In the Juncture Code, self-awareness is where everything must begin. Without self-awareness, how can you know if the decisions you're making align with your core values or your organization's goals? How can you recognize when your biases are creeping in or when your emotions are clouding your judgment? You can't. That's why self-awareness is the foundation of transformative leadership. But let's also be clear about what self-awareness is not. It is not about trying to be perfect—far from it. It's about having the courage to take an honest look at yourself and commit to ongoing growth. It's not always easy, but it's incredibly rewarding. Self-awareness isn't just another leadership buzzword; it's a proven predictor of success.

During my tenure as National Sales Director of Private Client Services for Wells Fargo Private Bank, I faced a career-changing moment that underscored the importance of self-awareness. At an executive meeting, I was tasked with restructuring the national leadership framework for the Licensed Banker and Store-Based Private Banker programs. The goal was to improve alignment and strengthen internal collaboration between the consumer bank and the private bank. This new structure would be critical to the future success of both businesses, as it represented a significant shift from how the two programs were managed. We were transitioning from a nationally centralized leadership model to regionally dispersed leadership teams positioned closer to local business units across the country.

The night before my presentation, I reviewed my slides and talking points, but something felt off. I remember a strange feeling in my stomach. Despite logic and data supporting my strategy, I couldn't shake the feeling that the consumer bank and regional leaders wouldn't fully embrace it. I paused and asked myself, "David, what's driving your approach? Are you truly aligned with the long-term needs of these businesses, or are you focusing more on persuasion than fostering connection and collaboration for transformation?" My answers led me to a realization that was humbling. I was trying to "sell" the strategy rather than involve the team in shaping it. I was neglecting the importance of shared ownership and aligned engagement. It was a big mistake driven by my own biases, and this moment of self-reflection had led me to see that and reset.

Instead of launching the meeting with a polished presentation, I opened with a story. I shared a time when I had failed to involve a team early in a critical decision, a misstep that resulted in misalignment and mistrust. I acknowledged the challenges ahead and invited the group to share their perspectives. This wasn't about presenting a perfect plan; it was about initiating honest dialogue. I watched the executives in front of me start to open up, and everything shifted. The ensuing discussion was richer, more collaborative, and more supportive than it would have been if I'd just told everyone my strategy. By the end, the strategy wasn't just mine—it was *ours*—and this would make all the difference as we moved forward through a complex, challenging, and crucial transition.

This experience reinforced a profound truth about the importance of self-reflection and self-awareness. By pausing to reflect on my own approach and biases, I was able to self-correct, lead with connection, and foster an environment that would ultimately lead to better outcomes. When leaders truly understand what is driving them, they gain clarity about their own biases, strengths, and weaknesses. This enables more purposeful behaviors and thinking.

Self-awareness isn't just about introspection; it's about ensuring your actions align with your personal values and organization's goals. This grounds leaders so they can navigate change and challenges with integrity and resilience. In practice, self-reflection and self-awareness impact every leadership moment. Knowing how your emotions and experiences influence your thinking allows you to respond thoughtfully rather than impulsively. This type of mindfulness fosters trust and connection, creating a culture where people feel understood, supported, and valued. People naturally gravitate toward leaders who are genuine and intentional, not just capable. Research consistently underscores this point.[132]

One of the biggest ways self-awareness improves leadership is through emotional intelligence. Daniel Goleman, a psychologist and bestselling author of several books on this topic, calls emotional intelligence the cornerstone of effective leadership, encompassing skills like empathy, social awareness, and self-regulation. It equips leaders to manage their own emotions, understand others, and build meaningful relationships—all skills that are critical in high-pressure situations.[133] Leaders with emotional intelligence are better at managing stress, staying composed in tough situations, and communicating in ways that resonate. Leaders grounded in self-awareness handle tough conversations with clarity, make balanced decisions, and create circumstances where everyone feels empowered. This creates an environment where teams feel supported and motivated to perform.

Another dimension of self-awareness, which I mentioned briefly, is recognizing unconscious biases. We're going to dive more deeply into assumptions and biases in Chapter 13. But for now, let's just recognize that everyone has blind spots when it comes to their own biases; it's the leaders who acknowledge and address them that create inclusive and equitable cultures. This introspective approach fosters not only an environment of fairness but also one of innovation and personal growth. Self-aware leaders create space for diverse perspectives where

---

[132]   Need original reference for this citation.

[133]   Goleman, D. (2006). *Emotional intelligence: Why it can matter more than IQ.* Bantam.

everyone's ideas are welcomed and valued. Moreover, self-aware leaders embrace feedback as a tool for growth, knowing that reflection and openness are the keys to continuous improvement.[134] This engenders ethical decision-making and reduces the risk of moral missteps.[135] When leaders lead with integrity, they inspire their teams to do the same, reinforcing a shared commitment to doing what's right.

There are many other benefits to self-awareness. Self-aware leaders are much more open to feedback. While hearing constructive criticism isn't always easy, these leaders actively seek it out, knowing it's essential for growth. Leaders who embrace feedback are more adaptable and better connected to their teams, creating an atmosphere of trust and mutual learning.[136] Adaptability is another key outcome of self-awareness. Leaders who know their strengths, weaknesses, principles, and values can adjust to challenges with confidence and clarity. This resilience ensures they can pivot effectively without losing sight of their goals.[137] This is the kind of leadership that not only plows through uncertainty but thrives in it.

Finally, self-awareness has a ripple effect. Leaders who are self-aware, authentic, and open create psychologically safe environments, where teams feel empowered to share ideas

---

[134] Brown, M. E., & Trevino, L. K. (2006). Ethical leadership: A review and future directions. The Leadership Quarterly, 17(6), 595-616. https://doi.org/10.1016/j.leaqua.2006.10.004

[135] Brown, M. E., & Trevino, L. K. (2006). Ethical leadership: A review and future directions. The Leadership Quarterly, 17(6), 595-616. https://doi.org/10.1016/j.leaqua.2006.10.004

[136] Eurich, T. (2018). *Insight: Why we're not as self-aware as we think, and how seeing ourselves clearly helps us succeed at work and in life.* Crown Business.

[137] Luthans, F., Avolio, B. J., & Avey, J. B. (2006). *Psychological capital: Developing the human competitive edge.* Oxford University Press.

and collaborate freely. This kind of culture fuels innovation, engagement, and success, proving that self-awareness isn't just a personal asset—it's an organizational advantage. When leaders model self-awareness, they set the tone for their people and their organizations. Authenticity and openness become cultural norms, creating a space where employees feel encouraged to share ideas, take risks, and engage fully. The result? A workplace filled with trust, creativity, and shared purpose. This manifests in innovation, high productivity and the ability to embrace meaningful change. This is the essence of effective leadership.

DEVELOP YOUR INNER COMPASS

Developing an inner compass means learning to use your own system of values, goals, and intuition to make decisions and navigate life. If your inner compass isn't fully developed, it's time for some deep self-reflection. You must ask yourself questions like this: "What are my core principles? What beliefs should guide my decisions?" For leaders, this work is necessary because your compass becomes a form of quiet authority. Instead of shouting for attention like your ego, your inner compass anchors you in truth when pressure, politics, and opinions threaten to pull you off your course.

When I reflect on my own leadership journey, I think back to that pivotal Wells Fargo moment when I was preparing to present a new plan for the national leadership structure. The night before, as I reviewed my carefully prepared slides, something felt off. Logic told me my data and arguments were solid, but my gut—my inner compass—was unsettled. That discomfort was self-awareness nudging me to pause and ask myself, "What's driving this decision?" Was I leading from connection or from persuasion? In that moment, I turned to my inner compass for direction. I realized I was trying to sell a strategy rather than co-create one. The next morning, instead of delivering the perfect plan, I invited conversation. That single act of alignment, between my values and behavior, changed everything. It shifted the tone from resistance to collaboration, and it reminded me that leadership isn't about proving you're right—it's about staying true to what matters most while bringing others with you.

This is what a leadership compass is all about. It's not a static list of values etched in stone; it's a living system that evolves as you grow and as your environment changes. The world you lead in today is the not the same world you led in five years ago, and your inner compass must adapt accordingly.

To build your inner compass, start by identifying three to five non-negotiable values that serve as your true north. These aren't just words like "honesty" or "teamwork," they are active commitments. For instance, if "transparency" is one of your values, how does that show up when you're under scrutiny or when the truth is inconvenient? If "courage" is core to who you are, how do you respond when courage requires vulnerability? Defining your values in the context of tension makes them real. It's easy to claim integrity when things are going well; it's hard, but far more meaningful, when integrity *costs* you something.

Once you've identified your anchors, test them through what I call values-under-stress scenarios. Picture yourself in a high-stakes moment: a board meeting gone sideways, a client conflict, or a public mistake. What would staying true to your values look like in that moment? What trade-offs might be asked of you and what pressures might you face? This kind of pre-reflection prepares you for real-world complexity. It strengthens emotional composure and moral clarity, the very capabilities that Daniel Goleman links to high emotional intelligence and effective leadership under pressure.[138]

PRACTICE MINDFULNESS

Equally important is practicing mindfulness on a daily basis. Neuroscience research shows that mindfulness strengthens the brain's prefrontal cortex, the region responsible for decision-making and impulse control.[139] Even brief pauses, a few deep breaths before a meeting or a moment of silence before a big decision, can help you tap into your inner compass for clarity and avoid reactivity. The act of slowing down helps you reconnect to your compass before speaking or acting, ensuring that your leadership is anchored in rational awareness rather than pure emotion.

Your compass also benefits from this calibration. Just as navigators compare their instruments against a true north, leaders need feedback to align perception with reality. Periodically ask trusted peers, mentors, or coaches, "What values do you see guiding my decisions? When do you notice I'm most aligned, or misaligned, with what I say matters?" This practice will not only sharpen your self-awareness, it will signal humility, an essential component of leadership.[140]

To make your compass more tangible, consider writing a leadership creed: a one-page statement that captures your core values, non-negotiables, and leadership promises. Mine includes commitments such as, "I will always engage others

---

[138] Goleman, D. (2006). *Emotional intelligence: Why it can matter more than IQ.* Bantam.

[139] We don't have a citation for this reference

[140] Eurich, T. (2018). *Insight: Why we're not as self-aware as we think, and how seeing ourselves clearly helps us succeed at work and in life.* Crown Business.

in shaping solutions rather than convincing them of mine," a lesson directly born from that Wells Fargo experience. A creed serves as both a declaration and a mirror, reminding you of the leader you aspire to be when circumstances threaten to pull you elsewhere.

Developing your inner compass is not a one-time event: it's a continual process of reflection, recalibration, and refinements. As the world changes, new challenges test your bearings. Each test is an opportunity to clarify what truly matters and to strengthen your capacity for authenticity. When your actions consistently align with your internal principles, your leadership takes on a sense of grounded presence. People trust you not because you have all the answers, but because they sense your steadiness: the quiet confidence of someone guided by conviction rather than convenience.

In the end, your inner compass is what allows you to lead through disruption without losing yourself. It is what transforms leadership from performance-driven to purpose-driven. And as your leadership expands, that compass not only guide you—it guides others who are watching, learning, and finding their own true north through your example.

KEY TAKEAWAYS

In today's complex workplace, self-awareness is more critical than ever. It's what allows leaders to stay grounded, connect meaningfully with their teams, and navigate challenges with purpose and clarity. By investing in self-awareness, leaders aren't just enhancing their own capabilities—they're building cultures of trust, resilience, and continuous improvement. Ultimately, a strong sense of self-awareness serves as a leader's foundation for navigating challenges and opportunities.

1. Self-awareness is the cornerstone of effective leadership, enabling leaders to align their decisions and actions with personal values and organizational goals, fostering trust and authenticity.

2. A well-tuned inner compass, developed through reflection and self-awareness, provides clarity and consistency, empowering leaders to navigate complexity with purpose and integrity.

3. Continuous self-reflection and openness to feedback enhance a leader's ability to adapt, make ethical decisions, and create an environment of trust and accountability within their teams.

CASE STUDY: WARREN BUFFETT'S COMMITMENT TO SELF-AWARENESS

Warren Buffett's legendary career isn't just about his financial savvy; it's deeply tied to his remarkable self-awareness and discipline. While many investors are tempted by the allure of quick wins or caught up in market hype, Buffett stands out for his unwavering commitment to his principles, his ability to recognize his own strengths and limitations, and his strategic, long-term perspective. One of Buffett's core principles is sticking to his "circle of competence" by focusing only on industries and businesses he truly understands. This isn't just smart investing; it's a profound example of self-awareness. Buffett knows where he excels and where he doesn't—and he's not afraid to admit it. Take the dot-com boom of the 1990s. While many investors chased tech stocks, Buffett stayed away, not because he wasn't interested, but because he didn't fully understand the technology sector at the time. This decision saved him from the losses many faced when the bubble burst. Later, after gaining a deeper understanding, he invested in companies like Apple, which became one of Berkshire Hathaway's most successful investments. It's a lesson in patience and staying true to what you know.[141]

Buffett's self-awareness extends to his values, which guide his every move. His philosophy of "value investing" is rooted in long-term thinking, buying strong companies with sustainable advantages rather than chasing short-term gains. This discipline reflects his inner compass, which keeps him focused on what truly matters, even when others are swayed by fleeting market trends. As Buffett famously said, "It's far better to buy a wonderful company at a fair price than a fair company at a wonderful price." His approach isn't just about numbers; it's about aligning investments with his belief in a company's durability and quality over the long haul.[142] It's a strategy that has consistently delivered results and earned him the trust of countless investors.

Buffett's self-awareness also shapes his leadership style. He knows his strengths but recognizes the importance of relying on others' expertise. At Berkshire Hathaway, he gives significant autonomy to his managers, trusting them to run their businesses independently. His motto, "Hire well, manage little," speaks volumes about his confidence in others and his understanding of the value of empowerment.[143] This trust-based approach has fostered a culture of accountability and loyalty at Berkshire Hathaway. Managers feel ownership of

141   Kilpatrick, A. (2008). *Of permanent value: The story of Warren Buffett.* Andy Kilpatrick Publishing.

142   Buffett, W. (1990). Letter to shareholders. Berkshire Hathaway Inc. Retrieved from https://www.berkshirehathaway.com/letters/1990.html

143   Buffett, W. (1989). Letter to shareholders. Berkshire Hathaway Inc. Retrieved from https://www.berkshirehathaway.com/letters/1989.html

their decisions, and the decentralized structure allows them to lead with confidence. Buffett's self-awareness here is key; he doesn't micromanage or pretend to know everything. Instead, he creates an environment where talented people can thrive.

But even Warren Buffett isn't immune to mistakes. In his annual letters to shareholders, he candidly discusses his errors, whether it's a bad acquisition or an investment that didn't pan out. This transparency not only reflects humility but also strengthens his credibility. His self-awareness helps him own failures and learn from them. He embraces mistakes as part of the growth process. By openly reflecting on his missteps, Buffett models a key leadership lesson: accountability matters.

Known for his modest lifestyle, Buffett is a living example of how values shape daily decisions and choices. His aversion to excess aligns with his core values of patience and prudence. This consistency enhances his credibility. It's hard not to respect a leader who practices what they preach, both in business and in life. His leadership is a lesson in self-awareness, discipline, and integrity.

REFLECTION

Ask yourself the following questions and write your answers in your journal. After, take time to reflect on your discoveries.

1. How clearly do I understand my core values, and how consistently do they guide my decisions?

2. In what ways do I leverage my strengths and address my weaknesses to improve my leadership?

3. How open am I to receiving and acting on feedback (Am I coachable?), and how does this impact my self-awareness?

4. Are there specific instances where my decisions or actions have conflicted with my stated values, and how can I realign?

5. How does my level of self-awareness influence the trust and collaboration within my team?

SELF-AUDIT

Rate yourself on a scale from one to ten, where one means "rarely or not at all" and ten means "frequently or very well."

1. I have a clear understanding of my core values and how they guide my leadership decisions.

    1   2   3   4   5   6   7   8   9   10

2. I am aware of my strengths and use them intentionally to enhance my leadership style.

    1   2   3   4   5   6   7   8   9   10

3. I recognize my weaknesses and actively work to address or mitigate them.

    1   2   3   4   5   6   7   8   9   10

4. I regularly reflect on my motivations, emotions, and decision-making processes.

    1   2   3   4   5   6   7   8   9   10

5. I am open to feedback and view it as an essential tool for improving self-awareness and growth.

    1   2   3   4   5   6   7   8   9   10

6. I can identify moments when my emotions or biases affect my decisions.

    1   2   3   4   5   6   7   8   9   10

7. I understand how my personal values influence my professional decisions and relationships.

   1   2   3   4   5   6   7   8   9   10

8. I take time to consider the long-term impact and alignment of my decisions with my goals.

   1   2   3   4   5   6   7   8   9   10

9. I am aware of biases that may shape my perceptions and actions, and I actively work to counteract them.

   1   2   3   4   5   6   7   8   9   10

10. I strive to consistently align my actions, decisions, and leadership style with my core values.

   1   2   3   4   5   6   7   8   9   10

EXERCISE: CREATE A SELF-AWARENESS JOURNAL

Develop a self-awareness journal dedicated to reflecting on your leadership journey. Use this as a space for intentional reflection and growth. At the end of each week, take twenty to thirty minutes to explore the following prompts:

1. **Key Decisions Made:** Reflect on one or two decisions you made. What motivated your choices, and how confident did you feel in their alignment with your values and goals?

2. **Emotional Awareness:** Recall moments when emotions played a role in your leadership. Were there times when emotions enhanced or hindered your decision-making? How did you respond?

3. **Values Alignment:** Consider how your actions reflected (or didn't reflect) your core values. Identify areas where you felt aligned and opportunities for improvement.

4. **Feedback Reflection:** Review feedback you received from your team, peers, or mentors. What does this feedback reveal about your strengths, blind spots, or areas for growth? How can you apply these insights?

5. **Insights and Lessons Learned:** Summarize any patterns you noticed or lessons you gained about your leadership, decision-making process, or how you approach challenges.

6. **Set Intentions:** Conclude by setting one small intention for the week ahead. For example:

    - "I will pause before reacting in emotionally charged situations."

    - "I'll seek feedback on a recent decision."

Over time, this journal will help you identify patterns, track your growth, and refine your inner compass, strengthening your self-awareness as a foundation for effective leadership.

CHAPTER 12

YOUR STRATEGIC APPROACH

"Strategy without analysis is a blind journey."

—Sun Tzu

I T WAS 1992, and I had been at PaineWebber in Nashville for about six months. By then, I had settled into the team, the office, and the city. As is often the case during transitions, the office was under pressure. Recruiters were circling, looking to take advantage of the uncertainty that comes with new leadership. Almost every one of my best financial advisors had enticing financial offers in their hands, creating a delicate situation.

In moments like these, there's always a risk of moving too fast. Many people assume new leadership will come in "with all the answers" and unintentionally disrupt the culture. Still, I knew I needed to act decisively. I approached the office's largest financial advisor, Mike Williams, and proposed a bold idea. I said, if he were open to coaching, we could double his results in three to four years.

It was a bold claim, and I knew it carried some risk. Mike was a top-tier producer focused on institutional fixed income, bringing in more than a million dollars in revenue annually. Yet it was clear that his business lacked structure, and it wasn't clear how effective his team performed. His processes were chaotic, and he was overlooking opportunities to expand into untapped markets that could dramatically increase his growth. In short, he was flying by the seat of his pants, relying on sheer determination rather than developing a strategic plan with defined processes to run his business.

As we began our conversation, Mike proudly highlighted the hard work he and his team had been putting in every day. I acknowledge their efforts and successes but told him I wanted to focus on something deeper. "You're clearly working hard *in* your business," I observed, "but how much time are you spending working *on* your business?" As it turned out, this was the question that changed everything. I was asking Mike to participate in strategic analysis and tactical business planning. Strategic analysis is the process of evaluating an organization's internal and external environments to understand its current state and future potential and it applies to both large and small businesses—like a financial advisor trying to take their business to the next level. Strategic planning uses the insights from this analysis to develop a roadmap for achieving organizational goals instead of operating on instinct.

My questions had shifted our conversation, and Mike said he was open to the process. Together, we began to examine every aspect of his practice, his top clients, growth trends, team responsibilities, and long-term goals. The more we analyzed, the clearer the picture became. His success, while impressive, was fragile, built on hustle and determination rather than strategy. What followed was a complete transformation. We developed a roadmap and segmented his client base to identify relationships that could open doors to new business. We redefined his team's roles, streamlining operations and freeing him to focus on his highest-value activities. Most importantly, we established a vision for his business's future and aligned every decision with that vision. The results were staggering. Within four years, Mike and his team tripled their business, becoming the largest financial advisor team in the country at PaineWebber. His practice expanded to include institutional equity, managed money advisory services, and financial planning for key clients. His team operated with newfound confidence and efficiency, his client relationships deepened, and his business grew in ways he never thought possible.

This experience reinforced a profound truth: success without strategy is precarious. Strategic analysis and planning aren't just for fixing troubled businesses, they also elevate good businesses into great ones. For this advisor, the shift was transformative. It wasn't just about working harder; it was about courageously stepping out of his comfort zone, which was fortified from the success he achieved, redefining his business, running his business like a business, and embracing what was possible as a result of strategic analysis.

THE POWER OF THE PAUSE

Mike had the courage to pause to take a step back from activity and assess his business. Because he did, he realized success he didn't believe was possible. That's the power of the pause. As the saying goes: sometimes you have to slow down to speed up. This is true in many aspects of business, but especially when the path forward looks anything but clear. Leadership is filled with moments where the stakes are high, and the right choice isn't obvious. That's why pausing for strategic analysis and planning is so crucial. It's how effective leaders make decisions rooted in long-term thinking rather than gut reactions or short-term fixes. Strategic analysis gives leaders the discipline to evaluate risks and opportunities from all angles while keeping the focus on the broader mission. Michael Porter has described this as, "balancing internal strengths with external forces"—a process that ensures decisions are deliberate, not reactive.[144]

One of the best things about strategic analysis is how it shifts your mindset. Instead of being consumed by short-term challenges, it trains you to think about long-term success. Leaders who embrace this approach aren't just putting out fires—they're building futures that can withstand uncertainty and change. And yet, as we'll explore next, clarity alone is rarely enough. Once leaders can *see clearly*, they must also learn to *see differently*. That's where possibility thinking begins.

WHAT IS YOUR STRATEGIC APPROACH?

Leadership without analysis is guesswork—and in a world of accelerating change, guesswork is a liability. Strategic analysis is not simply about dissecting information, it's about learning to see clearly, think deeply, and imagine broadly. At its best, it combines **analytical clarity**, **critical thinking**, and **possibility expansion**—three interconnected disciplines that form the foundation of intelligent leadership.

These elements work in sequence and in synergy. **Analytical clarity** helps you understand what already is, while **critical thinking** challenges you to discern what's true, and **expanding your options** by mapping untested paths empowers you to

---

[144] Porter, M. E. (1996). What is strategy? *Harvard Business Review*, 74(6), 61–78.

imagine what could be. Together, they give leaders a cognitive map for navigating uncertainty—the logic to evaluate, the courage to question, and the creativity to innovate. The most effective leaders don't stop once the data is organized and conclusions drawn; they pause again to explore. They use their clarity as a launching pad for curiosity, leveraging logic and imagination in equal measure. This dynamic interplay between evidence and exploration is what turns strategy from a static plan into a living discipline.

When practiced this way, strategic analysis becomes far more than just a leadership tool—it becomes a completely new way of thinking. It encourages leaders to see patterns others overlook, question assumptions others accept, and generate options others never consider. It demands reflection before reaction and imagination before decision. But let's be clear, analysis doesn't end with spreadsheets and reports. A developed strategy becomes real only when it meets execution.

SEEING WHAT MATTERS MOST

To understand what matters most as a leader, you must have analytical clarity—the ability to understand and express ideas, concepts, or data in a clear, precise, and comprehensible way, often by breaking down complex information into its logical components. It's the ability to filter out distractions, identify what's truly relevant, and translate complex information into clear priorities.

In a world overwhelmed by noise, clarity is your competitive advantage. When leaders achieve analytical clarity, they stop reacting to surface-level symptoms and start addressing root causes. They shift from reacting to anticipating, from busyness to outcomes. This clarity gives direction not only to decisions but to people, helping teams understand where to aim their energy and why it matters. To build analytical clarity, leaders must adopt the mindset of a systems thinker, seeing how parts connect rather than analyzing them in isolation. Whether evaluating market dynamics, customer behavior, or team performance, the question isn't just "What's happening?" but "What patterns are emerging and how do they influence what we do next?"

Use this reflective practice weekly or during major decision cycles.

1. **Clarify the Question:** Before diving into data, write down the one core question you're truly trying to answer. What problem are we *really* solving?

2. **Segment the Information:** List the top five categories of information available. Eliminate or deprioritize anything that doesn't directly support the question you clarified.

3. **Apply the 80/20 Rule:** Identify the 20% of information or actions that will drive 80% of the outcome. Be ruthless about removing what doesn't matter.

4. **Identify Interdependencies:** Draw a quick diagram showing how decisions in one area might influence another (e.g., talent > operations > customer experience).

5. **Summarize in One Sentence:** Condense your findings into a single sentence beginning with: "What this *really* means is . . ." This step forces clarity and clarity fuels intelligent action.

Repeat this process consistently and you'll begin to see connections that others miss.

Once you achieved analytical clarity, it's time to pursue disciplined curiosity—which is more formally called **critical thinking**. This is when you ask, "Why?" "What if?" and "What else?" It's the pathway from analysis to action. In leadership, it's not enough to identify data—you must interpret meaning, weigh alternatives, and anticipate consequences. This type of thinking helps to avoid the trap of "analysis paralysis" by moving from gathering information to making reasoned judgments.

Critical thinkers are challengers by nature. They resist easy answers, question assumptions, and look for disconfirming evidence before making major decisions. Daniel Kahneman's research on cognitive biases reminds us that even experienced leaders fall prey to overconfidence, anchoring, or confirmation bias. To counter these traps, you must slow down your thinking and deliberately challenge your own conclusions.

Strong critical thinkers use frameworks that blend both sides of the brain: analytical reasoning (logic, data, evidence) and creative reasoning (intuition, foresight, scenario planning). By combining both, leaders transform information into insight, and insight into intelligent action. Practice these steps when you face a major decision or strategic crossroad.

1. **List Your Assumptions**
    Write down the top three assumptions you are making about the issue or opportunity. Then, for each one, ask: What if this isn't true?

2. **Play Devil's Advocate**
    Ask a trusted peer or advisor to argue the opposite side of your conclusion.

    What points did they raise that you may have missed?

3. **Scenario Swap**

   Imagine two radically different outcomes: one wildly successful, one a complete failure. What decisions or conditions would lead to each? What can you learn from that contrast?

4. **Seek Dissent**

   In team discussions, assign one person to challenge the majority view. Reward them for identifying blind spots.

5. **Pause Before Action**

   Once your plan is formed, take a deliberate twenty-four-hour pause. Self-reflect by asking yourself, "Am I convinced because it's right, or because it's comfortable?"

These simple disciplines create the mental spacing that prevents reactionary thinking and strengthens leadership foresight.

TURNING CLARITY INTO POSSIBILITY

Once you've completed the critical thinking phase, you've earned the right to explore possibilities. This is where the creative side of leadership begins. Too many leaders stop at analysis; they define what it is but never imagine what could be. Expanding your options means turning insight into imagination. It's the deliberate process of exploring multiple pathways before committing to a single strategy. You use what you've learned through analysis not to narrow your vision, but to broaden it responsibly. Ask yourself:

- What are three radically different ways we could approach this problem?

- If we had no constraints, what would we try?

- What assumptions are limiting what I believe is possible?

The purpose of expanding options isn't to overcomplicate strategy, it's to prevent strategic blindness. When you develop a range of potential actions, you improve flexibility, creativity, and risk awareness. Analysis clarifies; imagination multiplies. By expanding your options, you create a bridge between insight and innovation—a space where data meets creativity and structured thinking gives rise to possibility. Practice Strategic Possibility Thinking as part of your strategic clarity and:

1. **Reframe the Question**
   Take a current challenge and restate it three different ways. Each reframing should open a new direction for exploration.

2. **Conduct a Pre-Mortem**
   Imagine a future where your current strategy failed. What would have caused it? Now reverse-engineer those insights to strengthen your plan.

3. **Engage in Option Storming**
   Instead of brainstorming solutions, brainstorm *options*. Quantity first, evaluation later. Aim for at least ten, because your best idea often comes after the first five.

4. **Rank for Range**
   Once you have your list, categorize options by range: *incremental*, *transformational*, and *unconventional*. Choose one from each category to explore further.

5. **Document Learnings**
   Write down the trade-offs, risks, and potential outcomes for each path. This practice ensures that creativity remains connected to disciplined decision-making.

Strategic planning is the moment when insight turns into movement; where analysis, reflection, and dialogue evolve into tangible, measurable action. It's the connection between knowing and doing—the phase where leadership becomes visible. Strategic analysis gives you awareness; strategic planning gives you momentum. And when done well, it transforms ideas into systems that create real results. Yet there's a hidden risk in this process, a subtle but dangerous loop that traps even the smartest teams: *think–plan–meet–repeat.* They analyze, refine, discuss, and polish their plans endlessly but never quite move forward. The work feels productive because it's full of collaboration and activity, but no true progress occurs. This overreliance on planning can quietly suffocate innovation and agility. This is often the difference between preparing for the future and perpetually preparing to prepare.

Leaders must remember that planning is not progress. You learn by doing. You adapt by acting. There's no such thing as a flawless strategy—only strategies that evolve through testing, feedback, and adjustment. The most effective leaders build enough structure to guide execution but not so much that it prevents experimentation. They know that motion creates clarity. Strategic planning operates as a cycle of intent > action > reflection > refinement. You clarify direction, you execute with discipline, and then you learn from what unfolds.

As Mintzberg and Senge both emphasized in their work on emergent strategy and learning organizations, strategy lives not in the plan itself but in the learning that execution generates.[145] Planning without execution is theory; execution without

---

[145]   Mintzberg, H. (1994). *The rise and fall of strategic planning.* The Free Press.

reflection and flexibility can lead to scattered outcomes. Real leadership exists in the balance between the two. The best organizations institutionalize this balance through feedback loops: formal moments to review, learn, and recalibrate based on real outcomes. These loops transform mistakes into data and data into better decisions. In essence, every plan becomes a prototype, refined through practice. Strategic planning, therefore, isn't about designing a perfect future—it's about building the courage and discipline to shape it in real time. When leaders treat planning as a living, adaptive process rather than a static ritual, they ignite momentum and create a culture that values progress over perfection, curiosity over certainty, and learning over control. That's how leaders move from thinking to thriving; one deliberate, adaptive step at a time.

BRINGING THE STEPS TOGETHER

Strategic analysis, critical thinking, and expanding your options form a leadership trilogy: clarity, challenge, and creativity. Together, they prevent tunnel vision, strengthen decision-making, and foster innovation. The intelligent leader doesn't stop at clarity—they push forward into curiosity, refusing to settle for a single option. They explore possibilities before they choose, and when they act, they do so with conviction grounded in analysis and imagination. That's how great leaders turn information into intelligence and intelligence into progress.

KEY TAKEAWAYS

In the end, strategic analysis, planning, and possibility design are more than leadership tools. Combined, they are a stabilizing force that anchors leaders in times of change and uncertainty by providing an integrated discipline that transforms insight into action. As Mike's transformation illustrates, analysis without imagination limits growth, and

   DAVID L ZIMMERMAN, MSC, CPC

imagination without structure limits execution. When you combine the rigor of strategic analysis with the openness of expanding possibilities, you unlock a leadership advantage rooted in both clarity and creativity. This is what separates reactive managers from visionary leaders: the ability to pause, assess, and imagine before acting.

Leaders who practice this balance navigate complexity with confidence, continuously refine their strategies through learning, and lead their teams through change with purpose and stability. Over time, these habits shape not just effective plans, but resilient, innovative cultures capable of thriving amid uncertainty.

1. Strategic *clarity* gives leaders the structure to assess reality, while strategic *imagination* empowers them to explore what's possible; together, they form the foundation of an adaptive style of leadership.

2. Leaders who integrate analysis, creativity, and disciplined planning make better decisions under pressure and cultivate agility within their teams.

3. Expanding your range of strategic options before committing to action ensures that choices are informed by both data and imagination, leading to more resilient outcomes.

4. By combining critical thinking and possibility thinking, leaders create a feedback loop of continuous improvement: learning, adapting, and innovating with intention.

5. The ability to stabilize through structure and grow through curiosity is the mark of modern leadership—anchored in clarity, yet open to reinvention.

CASE STUDY: HOW JACK WELCH USED STRATEGIC ANALYSIS AT GE

Jack Welch's tenure as CEO of General Electric (GE) is often cited as one of the most impactful applications of strategic analysis in corporate history.[146]

When Welch assumed leadership in 1981, GE was a large but sprawling conglomerate with multiple business units that were underperforming relative to their potential. Welch recognized that GE's wide range of businesses made it vulnerable to inefficiency, misallocation of resources, and strategic drift. His solution was to implement the famous "number one or number two" rule, requiring each GE business unit to rank either first or second in its industry, or face restructuring or divestiture.[147] This rule was not arbitrary; it was based on rigorous strategic analysis and an in-depth understanding of market dynamics. Welch knew that focusing on competitive positioning would allow GE to concentrate its efforts on businesses with the potential to achieve and sustain leadership positions. His approach involved comprehensive assessments of each unit's strengths, weaknesses, opportunities, and threats—a framework later popularized as the SWOT analysis.[148]

Welch and his team delved deeply into each business's competitive landscape, examining factors such as market share, growth potential, innovation capacity, and financial performance. This meticulous approach led to a series of strategic divestitures, freeing up resources that were then redirected to high-potential

---

[146] Need reference for this citation.

[147] Welch, J., & Byrne, J. A. (2001). *Jack: Straight from the gut.* Warner Business Books.

[148] Need reference for this citation.

business units.[149] Beyond restructuring, Welch's strategic vision extended to fostering a culture of accountability and data-driven decision-making at GE. He emphasized that every decision must be anchored in hard data, with measurable outcomes tied to the company's broader strategic goals. Business unit leaders were expected to adopt the same rigorous analytical framework Welch used, instilling a mindset where strategic analysis was not just a corporate initiative but a fundamental part of GE's culture. This emphasis on analytics enabled GE to consistently achieve disciplined growth, innovation, and profitability, even as market conditions evolved.[150]

Welch also looked outward and imagined new possibilities by emphasizing what he called "boundaryless behavior," which encouraged open communication and collaboration across GE's business units. He believed that by breaking down silos, GE could achieve a flow of information that would further enhance strategic analysis, allowing different divisions to share insights, market intelligence, and best practices. This cross-collaborative approach amplified GE's strategic agility, which supported the company's positioning to pivot based on shared knowledge, rather than isolated decision-making.

One of Welch's notable applications of strategic analysis was the acquisition and integration of RCA, a major electronics and broadcasting company, in 1986. Although the acquisition was a departure from GE's core industrial focus, Welch's team conducted thorough due diligence and strategic analysis to ensure RCA's alignment with GE's long-term goals. RCA's

---

[149] Slater, R. (1999). *Jack Welch and the GE way: Management insights and leadership secrets of the legendary CEO.* McGraw-Hill.

[150] Tichy, N. M., & Sherman, S. (1993). *Control your destiny or someone else will: How Jack Welch is making General Electric the world's most competitive company.* Doubleday.

profitable television broadcasting business, including NBC, complemented GE's strategic vision, offering a robust revenue stream and bolstering GE's capabilities in a new industry. However, Welch's commitment to performance led him to divest RCA's consumer electronics division shortly after, once strategic analysis revealed that it lacked the potential to become a market leader, a move that underscored his disciplined, results-oriented approach to decision-making.[151]

Welch's strategic philosophy did not merely transform GE—it became a case study in effective corporate leadership and strategic management. His commitment to systematic, data-driven analysis created a template for countless organizations that recognized the need for discipline in decision-making. His legacy demonstrated that strategic analysis is not simply a management tool, but a cultural foundation for sustainable success. By embedding this disciplined approach into GE's DNA, Welch positioned the company to remain resilient and adaptable in the face of evolving market challenges, leaving a lasting impact on both GE and the broader business world.[152] His disciplined, data-driven approach and focus on aligning decisions with GE's strategic priorities offer valuable lessons for leaders seeking to navigate complex challenges with clarity and purpose.

REFLECTION

Ask yourself the following questions and write your answers in your journal. After, take time to reflect on your discoveries.

---

[151] Welch, J., & Byrne, J. A. (2001). *Jack: Straight from the gut.* Warner Business Books.

[152] Slater, R. (1999). *Jack Welch and the GE way: Management insights and leadership secrets of the legendary CEO.* McGraw-Hill.

   DAVID L ZIMMERMAN, MSC, CPC

Analytical Reflection

1. When facing complex challenges, do I take the time to pause and analyze before reacting?

2. How often do I validate my assumptions with data instead of opinions or intuition?

3. Do I have a repeatable process for evaluating risk and opportunities objectively?

4. Dow well do I balance my instincts with evidence-based reasoning when making key decisions?

5. After major decisions, do I revisit what worked, what didn't, and what I learned in the process?

Exploratory Reflection

6. Once I have analytical clarity, do I actively explore alternative paths before finalizing a plan?

7. Do I encourage my team to challenge my assumptions and offer unconventional ideas?

8. How comfortable am I embracing uncertainty while designing new options?

9. Do I routinely engage in scenario planning or creative what-if discussions to widen my perspective?

10. When developing strategies, do I ensure our options represent innovation, not just optimization?

Rate yourself on a scale from one to ten, where one means "rarely or not at all" and ten means "frequently or very well."

1. I regularly pause to analyze before making big decisions.

1	2	3	4	5	6	7	8	9	10

2. I question whether current success might limit future growth.

1	2	3	4	5	6	7	8	9	10

3. I intentionally seek input from people who think differently.

1	2	3	4	5	6	7	8	9	10

4. I test ideas through action rather than endless discussion.

1	2	3	4	5	6	7	8	9	10

5. I balance logic and imagination when evaluating new paths.

1	2	3	4	5	6	7	8	9	10

6. I actively challenge my own data interpretations when evaluating new paths.

1	2	3	4	5	6	7	8	9	10

7. I can articulate at least three future scenarios for my organization or business unit.

1	2	3	4	5	6	7	8	9	10

8. When evaluating strategy, I consider both measurable outcomes and cultural impact.

1	2	3	4	5	6	7	8	9	10

9. I make time to re-evaluate past decisions, identifying what I learned rather than just focusing on whether it succeeded.

 DAVID L ZIMMERMAN, MSC, CPC

1   2   3   4   5   6   7   8   9   10

10. I foster an environment where experimentation and learning from failure are valued as part of the strategic process.

1   2   3   4   5   6   7   8   9   10

EXERCISE: SCENARIO PLANNING

1. **Identify a Current Strategic Decision**
   Choose a leadership challenge or decision that requires careful analysis. This could be a project launch, organizational restructuring, or a decision about resource allocation.
2. Define what's true: What do you know with certainty?
3. Define what's unknown: What variables or assumptions could shift?
4. **Outline Three Potential Scenarios**
   Develop three distinct scenarios for how the situation might unfold:

   - Optimistic Scenario: What happens if everything goes better than expected?

   - Neutral Scenario: What happens under standard conditions?

   - Pessimistic Scenario: What happens if major challenges arise?

5. **Analyze Each Scenario**
   For each scenario, answer the following questions:

   - What are the key risks and opportunities?

   - What resources will be needed?

○ How does this align with your organizational goals?

6. **Evaluate Strategic Actions**
Based on the scenarios, identify two or three strategic actions for each scenario. Consider how these actions will address risks and maximize opportunities.

7. **Reflect on Decision Alignment**
After completing the analysis, reflect on:

   ○ How does your decision align with your long-term goals?

   ○ What insights did you gain from analyzing different outcomes?

   ○ How will you incorporate this approach into future strategic challenges?

By completing this exercise, you'll gain a clearer understanding of how different outcomes can shape your decision-making process. It's not just about preparing for the best or worst-case scenario—it's about building the confidence to approach challenges with a well-rounded perspective.

CHAPTER 13

CHALLENGE ASSUMPTIONS AND BIASES

"The greatest enemy of knowledge is not ignorance;
it is the illusion of knowledge."

—Stephen Hawking

I T W A S M A R C H 2003, and I had just accepted a chief-of-staff role to the president of the Los Angeles Bank for Wells Fargo. My team would include marketing, sales, events, and training for branch managers, store-based private bankers and licensed bankers. My first directive was clear: turn around the marketing department. I entered the role full of confidence, armed with what I believed were tried-and-true strategies for success. I'd led similar teams before, so I assumed I knew the challenges.

"We need to focus on efficiency—and that's going to take both restructuring and completely reworking our processes," I'd told my leadership team during our first meeting. "Let's streamline processes, prioritize high-value client projects for visibility, and boost support for our branch network. That's how we're going to win." Everyone nodded along. I didn't think to ask for feedback because I assumed their nods meant agreement. After all, my approach had worked before. Why wouldn't it work here? Boy, was I in for a valuable lesson in leadership!

Over the next few months, we implemented changes quickly. We revamped workflows, adjusted areas of responsibility, and even moved the entire marketing department from the San Diego area to Los Angeles. At first, the energy was high. The changes were met with cautious optimism. Everyone wanted to believe we were on the right path. But then the cracks began to show.

A few leaders approached me privately to share concerns. "This isn't working for us," one admitted. "We're spending more time on systems and processes than delivering creative work that will set us apart with our clients." Another reported, "You're treating this office like the last one you led, but our challenges are different." I listened to their feedback—but the truth was that I'd been brought in to fix problems, and I believed I was doing exactly that. "Just give it time," I responded somewhat dismissively. "These types of changes take some time to kick in."

It wasn't long before I could no longer ignore the warning signs. Things were not improving, morale was slipping, and I discovered that some of my best people were quietly considering offers from our competitors. Something had gone wrong, but I didn't know what. Then, one morning, during a routine review, the head of marketing made a comment that hit me like a freight train. "David, you haven't actually asked any of us what we think we need. You just assumed you knew." Ouch! I didn't know how to respond. I probably looked like a deer in the headlights. I had come to this role with a successful playbook of solutions and imposed them on my teams without pausing to fully understand the unique challenges these people faced. I assumed their problems mirrored those of my previous teams. I assumed I already had the answers. I was wrong.

The next day, I called a full team meeting. This time, I didn't come with answers. I came with an apology and a bunch of questions. "Tell me what you're seeing. What's holding us back?" I asked. "What do you need to be successful?" What followed was a humbling and powerful experience. Most people on the team spoke candidly about the dynamics unique to our region. They explained that our clients lived throughout the city in micro-markets with vast differences in culture and income. This created unique segmentation challenges. The sweeping, one-size-fits-all changes I'd implemented had inadvertently undermined the creative solutions marketing was trying to deliver to this diverse client base.

Over the next few weeks, we rebuilt our strategy together. We kept the changes that worked and scrapped what didn't. We refocused on deepening relationships and creating strategies tailored to this team's strengths and weaknesses. By listening first and recognizing my false assumptions, I gave the team a voice and regained their trust. In the end, we managed to turn things around—not because I imposed my solutions, but because I worked with the team to find the right solutions for this organization and its people.

It was a masterclass in why leaders should always question their assumptions and analyze potential biases. Leadership is full of challenges that demand clear, innovative thinking, but here's the catch: our own assumptions can sometimes hold us back. These assumptions, often operating quietly in the background, have the power to cloud our judgment, limit our creativity, and create blind spots we don't even realize are there. That's why the ability to question assumptions is such a critical leadership skill. By examining our own thought patterns and challenging the beliefs we may have taken for granted, we can make decisions that are not only smarter, but also more inclusive and forward-looking.

This step in the Juncture Code—challenging assumptions and biases—gives leaders the tools to step outside of habitual thinking and see the bigger picture. It's about creating the space to ask, "What if I'm wrong?" or "What am I missing?" These are simple but transformative questions that open the door to better insights, more creative solutions, and a leadership style that's flexible and adaptable.

Let's consider once again how often decisions are shaped by biases we don't even notice. These mental shortcuts might feel familiar and comfortable, but they can block progress by skewing our ability to see the objective bigger picture. When leaders make a habit of questioning their own decision-making, they're setting an example for their teams. Encouraging a culture of curiosity and critical thinking inspires everyone to approach problems with fresh eyes. In this chapter, we'll explore how breaking free from assumptions can boost your leadership effectiveness, spark innovation, and help you adapt to an ever-changing world.

QUESTIONING AS A CATALYST

When leaders take the time to step back and challenge ingrained beliefs, they open the door to innovation and growth. Too often, assumptions are shaped by past successes, cultural norms, or deeply held habits that haven't been revisited in years. By breaking free from these limiting patterns, leaders can expand their strategic vision and discover opportunities that might otherwise remain hidden. Questioning your assumptions doesn't just benefit you as a leader, it transforms entire organizations.

In his book, *The Fifth Discipline*, Peter Senge takes the concept of psychological safety even further with the concept of a "learning organization."[153] He argues that organizations thrive when they foster a culture of continuous learning and critical thinking. This means not just questioning what works, but actively seeking out what could work better. When leaders and teams embrace this approach, they're more agile and better prepared to navigate uncertainty and change. For the Juncture Code, challenging assumptions is more than a per-project exercise—it's a way of thinking that builds resilience and adaptability. Leaders who make this a habit signal their commitment to growth, openness, and collaboration. This builds an organizational culture primed for sustainable success. Ronald Heifetz and Marty Linsky, both prominent figures in the field of adaptive leadership, emphasize that this ability to adapt and rethink is what separates thriving organizations from those that fall behind.[154]

Think of challenging assumptions as a team sport. When leaders encourage open dialogue, they invite their teams to bring fresh perspectives and uncover hidden blind spots. This doesn't just lead to better decisions—it drives continuous improvement, helping teams stay ahead of industry trends and

---

[153] Senge, P. M. (2006). *The Fifth Discipline: The Art & Practice of The Learning Organization*. Doubleday.

[154] Heifetz, R., & Linsky, M. (2002). *Leadership on the Line: Staying Alive through the Dangers of Leading*. Harvard Business Press.

shifting landscapes. It's a dynamic, ongoing process that keeps your leadership, and your organization, relevant and resilient. This collective progress builds a foundation for long-term success, equipping organizations to tackle challenges with flexibility, creativity, and confidence.

BECOME A BIAS BREAKER

Let's talk about what it means to be a "Bias Breaker." Being a Bias Breaker is not just about spotting biases; it's about committing to a systematic approach where you actively challenge them—yours and others. Biases, whether conscious or unconscious, are those mental shortcuts that sneak into our thinking, shaping how we see the world and make decisions. While they can sometimes help us make snap decisions in high-stress situations, they often cloud judgment and lead to decisions that are not sustainable over time. As a Bias Breaker, you're committing to saying, "I'm not going to let unchecked assumptions run the show here." Instead, you're committing to clarity, intentionality, and intellectual rigor in every decision you and your team make. This mindset is all about disrupting the autopilot that often governs our thinking and decision-making. When you put on your Bias Breaker hat, you create space for yourself and your team to question the status quo. It's not about being combative; it's about encouraging curiosity, asking better questions, digging deeper, and welcoming perspectives that challenge your own and others. Leaders who embody this approach don't just make better decisions—they create an environment where innovation, adaptability, and growth flourish.

In chapter five, we explored how biases shape our thinking. Here, we shift from awareness to activation—building the habits and practices that challenge both biases and the broader assumptions they feed. Here's the best part: adopting a Bias

Breaker approach doesn't require an overhaul of your leadership style. It's simply about developing intentional habits that sharpen your awareness.

1. **Identify Your Biases and Assumptions**

   To tackle biases, you first need to notice them first. We talked about being mindful of our biases and assumptions in the self-awareness chapter. But this needs to become a leadership discipline. Awareness takes practice throughout the day and in a variety of situations. You bring different biases and assumptions to different groups, situations, and challenges. Maybe a recent experience created a new bias. The only assumption you should always make is that everyone, including you, is always bringing baggage to the conference table, and it needs to be checked in order for constructive innovation and problem-solving to take place. Find simple, repeatable ways to remind yourself to stop and recognize potential biases and assumptions. Practicing mindfulness—whether through short pauses during your day, reflective journaling, or something else to help you tune into your thoughts and reactions—is a great strategy that will help you see things more objectively and, if necessary, quickly course correct. Research shows that this increases cognitive flexibility, making it easier to catch those moments when a bias might be steering your decisions.[155] And after every key decision, stop for a moment and ask yourself, "What assumptions was I working with here?" or "Did my emotions influence this choice in any way?"

---

[155] Dane, E. (2011). Paying attention to mindfulness and its effects on task performance in the workplace. *Journal of Management*, 37(4), 997-1018.

2. **Build a Cognitive Toolkit**

   Techniques like "consider the opposite" can be game-changers when it comes to spotting potential biases and assumptions—especially when reframing limiting beliefs, such as, "Well, that idea has never worked before!" As you lean toward a specific answer or solution in your decision-making process, make it a habit to ask yourself simple questions like, "What if the opposite were true?" This simple technique interrupts confirmation bias and forces you to see things from another angle.[156] Another great tool is the pre-mortem analysis.[157] Picture the decision going completely wrong and work backward to uncover what could have caused the failure. These techniques turn abstract thinking into actionable clarity. There are plenty of easy cognitive tools to change your patterns and become more cognizant of your biases and assumptions. Build your cognitive toolkit so you can be prepared for any situation. Consider making it a collaborative effort for team members to share their tools.

3. **Explore Diverse Perspectives**

   Your perspective is valuable, but it's definitely not the only one that matters. Inviting feedback from people with different experiences and expertise can uncover blind spots you didn't even know were there. Scott Page, the John Seely Brown Distinguished University Professor of Complexity, Social Science, and Management at the University of Michigan, found that diverse

---

[156] Lord, C. G., Lepper, M. R., & Preston, E. (1984). Considering the opposite: A corrective strategy for social judgment. *Journal of Personality and Social Psychology, 47*(6), 1231.

[157] Klein, G. (2007). Performing a project pre-mortem. *Harvard Business Review, 85*(9), 18-19.

teams consistently outperform homogenous ones in problem-solving because they approach challenges from multiple angles.[158] So, ask your team: "What am I missing here?" or "How would you approach this?" Their insights can reveal paths you hadn't considered.

4. **Create a Biases Journal**

   Tracking your biases and assumptions in a journal might sound like homework, but it's one of the simplest ways to build awareness. Take five to ten minutes each day to jot down and explore moments when you realize bias might have influenced your thinking. Over time, patterns will emerge, helping you understand the triggers that lead to snap judgments or poor decisions. Using prompts that specifically focus on disentangling subjective beliefs from objective reality will help in remarkable ways. Ask yourself, "What beliefs am I taking for granted?" or "What might someone with a different perspective say about this?" These questions can help reframe the snap-judgement thinking that is often inspired by cognitive bias. These prompts can guide your reflections and make bias-breaking a constructive new habit.

5. **Stay Humble**

   Being a Bias Breaker isn't about having all the answers; it's about being willing to admit when you're wrong and learn from it. Leaders who stay humble, or practice intellectual humility, invite feedback, revisit their assumptions, admit mistakes, and adapt to new information. This doesn't weaken your leadership; it

---

[158] Page, S. E. (2007). *The Difference: How the Power of Diversity Creates Better Groups, Firms, Schools, and Societies.* Princeton University Press.

strengthens it by showing your team that you hold yourself accountable because growth and learning should never stop.

Challenging biases isn't just about improving individual decisions; it's about creating a ripple effect throughout your team and organization. When you model openness, self-awareness, and curiosity, your team picks up on it. They feel empowered to question their own assumptions and biases, share ideas, and approach problems with fresh eyes and openness. This isn't just good for morale, it's a proven driver of innovation and resilience.[159] As a Bias Breaker, you're not just improving how you lead, you're creating a culture that's built to last. Your commitment to questioning, learning, and growing inspires those around you to do the same. This approach makes your organization more agile, more inclusive, and better equipped to thrive in a world that's constantly changing. So, the next time you're faced with a tough decision, ask yourself, "Am I seeing the full picture? What assumptions do I need to challenge?" The answers could be the key to unlocking your next big breakthrough.

KEY TAKEAWAYS

The benefits of this mindset are immense. By recognizing and challenging biases, leaders open themselves and their teams to new perspectives, better ideas, and solutions that might have otherwise been overlooked. They set the tone for a culture that values learning, flexibility, and growth—exactly the kind of culture that fuels long-term innovation. In the broader context of the Juncture Code, this approach aligns perfectly with the

---

[159] Edmondson, A. C. (2018). *The Fearless Organization: Creating Psychological Safety in the Workplace for Learning, Innovation, and Growth*. Wiley.

framework's focus on thoughtful, resilient decision-making. The lesson here is clear: cognitive biases aren't going away, but leaders can outsmart them. By bringing these hidden influences to light, and actively challenging them, leaders position themselves and their teams to think more clearly, innovate more boldly, and adapt more effectively to a world of constant change.

1. **Challenging Assumptions Unlocks Growth and Innovation**
   Leaders who question their own and their organization's assumptions create opportunities for innovation, uncovering new solutions and fostering a culture of adaptability and creativity.

2. **Bias Awareness Elevates Decision-Making**
   Recognizing and addressing cognitive biases like confirmation bias and status quo bias allows leaders to make more balanced, informed, and forward-thinking decisions, aligning with long-term goals.

3. **Being a Bias Breaker Promotes Openness**
   Developing a mindset dedicated to questioning deeply and embracing intellectual humility empowers leaders to remain flexible, foster diverse perspectives, and drive continuous improvement within their teams and organizations.

CASE STUDY: ALAN MULALLY AT FORD MOTOR COMPANY—BREAKING THE ILLUSION OF COMPETENCE

In 2006, when Alan Mulally left Boeing to become CEO of Ford Motor Company, the automaker was on the verge of collapse. Losses were mounting into the billions, and its once dominant market share was rapidly eroding. Inside the company, senior leaders clung to a dangerous illusion: the belief that Ford's problems were external, not internal. Every weekly report was coded "green," signaling that everything was on track, even though financial data told a very different story.[160] Mulally quickly recognized this illusion for what it was: an organizational bias rooted in fear and self-preservation. Executives had learned that bad news brought punishment, so they avoided transparency altogether. The culture of denial had become a form of collective blindness. Mulally described it as "the illusion of competence," the comforting but false notion that appearances of control equaled real control.[161]

Determined to expose this bias, Mulally launched a new ritual he called the Business Plan Review (BPR). Every Thursday, Ford's top leaders gathered around a conference table to review progress against key performance goals. Each executive was required to present a color-coded update: green for good, yellow for at-risk, and red for serious trouble. In the first meeting, every chart was green. Mulally looked around the room and asked calmly, "If we're losing billions, how can everything be green?" The silence was deafening.[162]

---

[160]   SupplyChainBrain. (2010, December 22). *Bad news bears the seeds of Ford's turnaround success.* SupplyChainBrain. *https://wwwsupplychainbrain.com/articles/9490-bad-news-bears-the-seeds-of-fords-turnaround-success*

[161]   SupplyChainBrain. (2010, December 22). *Bad news bears the seeds of Ford's turnaround success.* SupplyChainBrain. *https://wwwsupplychainbrain.com/articles/9490-bad-news-bears-the-seeds-of-fords-turnaround-success*

[162]   Kellog, D. (2022, March 8) Alan Mulally, Ford, and the 6Cs. Brookings Institution. *https://www.brookings.edu/articles/alan-mulally-ford-and-the-6cs/*

At the next meeting, one executive, Mark Fields, displayed a red chart for the first time. The room froze, expecting reprimand. Instead, Mulally clapped and said, "Great visibility, Mark. What can we do to help?" That moment shattered Ford's culture of fear. Mulally had challenged one of the company's most ingrained assumptions: that admitting failure equated to weakness. By reframing transparency as strength, he began rebuilding psychological safety inside the organization, a concept Amy Edmondson later described as foundational to innovation and adaptive performance.[163]

Mulally's approach reflected a deep understanding of adaptive leadership, the ability to confront uncomfortable truths and orchestrate learning across an organization under stress. He shifted the focus from protecting reputations to solving problems collectively. Over time, leaders began surfacing issues earlier, cross-functional collaboration replaced territorial thinking, and data replace defensiveness. By 2009, Ford was the only one of the "Big Three" U.S. automakers to avoid a federal bailout. The company returned to profitability, regained market confidence, and reignited employee pride.[164] More importantly, Mulally proved that challenging assumptions isn't an act of defiance—it's an act of integrity.

Ford's turnaround illustrates how dangerous hidden biases can be when left unchecked. The assumption that everything is fine is often leadership's most seductive lie. By exposing that illusion, Mulally modeled humility, courage, and curiosity: the core elements of bias-breaking leadership. His story reinforces a truth at the heart of the Juncture Code: organizations don't

---

[163] Edmondson, A. C. (2018). *The Fearless Organization: Creating Psychological Safety in the Workplace for Learning, Innovation, and Growth.* Wiley.

[164] Humes, E. (2012). *American Idol: Alan Mulally and the fight to save Ford Motor Company.* HarperBusiness.

transform because of better plans, they transform when leaders create the safety and discipline to confront reality, learn in public, and act with clarity.

REFLECTION

Ask yourself the following questions and write your answers in your journal. After, take time to reflect on your discoveries.

1. What assumptions do I regularly rely on in my decision-making, and how might they limit my perspective?

2. How do I create opportunities to challenge my own and my team's assumptions during critical decision-making moments?

3. What biases, such as confirmation or status quo bias, might be influencing my leadership decisions, and how can I address them?

4. How can I model intellectual humility and curiosity to inspire my team to question assumptions and think creatively?

5. In what ways can rethinking deeply held assumptions unlock new opportunities or drive innovation within my organization?

SELF-AUDIT

Rate yourself on a scale from one to ten, where one means "rarely or not at all" and ten means "frequently or very well."

1. I regularly question my own assumptions to ensure they align with the current context.

    1   2   3   4   5   6   7   8   9   10

2. I actively identify and address cognitive biases that may cloud my judgment.

   1   2   3   4   5   6   7   8   9   10

3. I foster an environment where my team feels safe to challenge assumptions and offer diverse perspectives.

   1   2   3   4   5   6   7   8   9   10

4. I seek out diverse viewpoints to broaden my understanding and inform my decision-making.

   1   2   3   4   5   6   7   8   9   10

5. I am open to revising my opinions and strategies based on new evidence or feedback.

   1   2   3   4   5   6   7   8   9   10

6. I critically evaluate whether established practices remain effective or need to evolve.

   1   2   3   4   5   6   7   8   9   10

7. I intentionally look for blind spots in my decision-making and leadership approach.

   1   2   3   4   5   6   7   8   9   10

8. I encourage my team to approach challenges with curiosity and a willingness to rethink assumptions.

   1   2   3   4   5   6   7   8   9   10

9. I actively seek feedback to uncover biases and improve my decision-making processes.

   1   2   3   4   5   6   7   8   9   10

10. I demonstrate intellectual humility by acknowledging when I'm wrong and learning from others.

EXERCISE: IDENTIFYING ASSUMPTIONS

Objective: to identify, evaluate, and challenge assumptions in your decision-making process, fostering critical thinking and enabling more informed, innovative outcomes.

Step 1: Select a Current Challenge

Choose a project, decision, or leadership scenario where assumptions play a significant role. This could be anything from a new strategy you're considering to team dynamics you're addressing.

Step 2: Identify Assumptions

Write down three key assumptions you hold about the challenge. For each assumption, ask:

- What do I believe to be true in this situation?

- Why do I hold this belief?

- Is this assumption based on facts, past experiences, or biases?

Step 3: Explore Biases and Influences

For each assumption, reflect on potential cognitive biases that may be influencing your thinking, such as:

- Confirmation Bias: Am I only seeking information that supports this belief?

- Status Quo Bias: Am I resisting change because it feels safer?

- Anchoring Bias: Is my judgment overly influenced by initial information?

   DAVID L ZIMMERMAN, MSC, CPC

Step 4: Develop Questions to Test Assumptions

Draft questions or experiments to challenge your assumptions. For example:

- What evidence would prove this assumption wrong?

- How might someone with a different perspective view this situation?

- What alternative approaches could address this challenge more effectively?

Step 5: Seek Input and Feedback

Share your assumptions and questions with trusted team members or mentors. Ask for their insights to uncover blind spots or alternative viewpoints.

Step 6: Reflect and Adjust

Based on your findings, reflect on how your assumptions have shaped your approach. Consider how modifying or letting go of certain assumptions can lead to better decisions or innovative solutions.

CHAPTER 14

EXECUTE WITH EXCELLENCE

"Vision without execution is hallucination."

—Thomas Edison

I T WAS 2021, and the complexities of COVID were well underway. As Head of Wealth Management for Atlantic Union Bank, I was presented with a challenge that perfectly encapsulated the difficulties of leadership and decision-making. The bank had acquired three registered investment advisory (RIA) businesses over the previous few years. On paper, the goal was clear: consolidate these distinct firms into a single cohesive business unit. In reality, each firm was unique in terms of culture, leadership style, and business approach. These and other factors intertwined with the bank turned the integration into a monumental task.

The responsibility of bringing these firms together fell to our chief investment officer, Sam. Brilliant at managing money and navigating the markets, he was a master of strategy when it came to portfolios and investments. However, merging three diverse organizations required a very different set of skills—ones rooted in leadership, operational strategy, and organizational change.

As the project unfolded, it became clear that the lack of a structured approach was creating confusion, slowing progress, and diluting accountability. One particular meeting brought the issue to a head. Leaders from the three firms sat around the table, each passionately advocating for their way of doing things. Discussions were all over the place—one moment focused on investment style, the next on client segmentation, and then compliance and operations. Juggling too many priorities and inputs, Sam had no clear plan for how to move forward. While he was a great listener and advocate, he found himself frozen on sequencing steps and accountability. It was a classic case of everyone trying to do everything, leaving no one focused on the most critical decisions. The moment called for clarity. I stepped in with questions for the group.

"Okay, everyone, I know this is challenging, but what *is the ultimate goal?*" The room went silent for a moment, and then people started to answer. I followed up. "This is great. We're making progress. I have another question: *Who owns which decisions?*"

This question also caused everyone to pause. Both questions cut through the noise and forced us all to take a step back and focus. We recognized that the integration effort needed a more defined structure and clear accountability. Without these, progress would remain elusive, and success would slip through our fingers. I worked with the entire team to reset the approach. First, we articulated the vision: a unified RIA business that captured the best of each legacy firm while aligning with the Wealth Management Group's broader goals. Then, we conducted a strategic analysis, and based on our findings, outlined our strategic priorities: cohesion with investment styles, aligning leadership structures, and streamlining operations and compliance processes. Most importantly, we worked on our roadmaps and defined roles, responsibilities, and resource allocations. This recalibration marked a turning point. With clear decision-makers assigned to each priority, the team could focus their efforts rather than spread themselves thin. Progress accelerated. Redundancies were eliminated, a unified leadership structure was established, and investment policies and procedures began to take shape. By the end of the year, the three firms were becoming a cohesive unit, positioned for growth and greater client impact.

This experience reinforced my belief in the importance of the Juncture Code. The event showed me that before you can execute effectively, you need to follow all the steps of the Juncture Code and get to the point where you have a well-developed business plan, complete with clear measurement and accountability. Without this roadmap, even the best teams, with the best intentions, will falter.

When everyone tries to do everything, no one does anything (well). Priorities, grounded in clarity and alignment, are the foundation for success. As a leader, you have to create focus and execute with precision. Leadership isn't about tackling every challenge at once or allowing priorities to remain ambiguous—it's about focusing on what matters most, ensuring decisions are aligned with overarching goals, and empowering the right people to take action. Making decisions that create focus is one of the most critical skills a leader can develop. It's not just about picking the "right" option, it's about making intentional decisions that are aligned with the mission and strategy.

Up until this point, we've focused on building a strong foundation for navigating challenges and changes. Now, all that preparation comes into play. It's time to focus on *execution*, where insight meets action. The ability to execute your decisions is essential—not just for navigating challenges, but for steering your team and organization towards its long-term, strategic goals.

The most effective leaders do the necessary strategic analysis and planning so they can execute with clarity, focus, and confidence. Research shows that when leaders pair structured decision-making and planning with a focused commitment to their objectives, they position themselves and their organizations for success, particularly in environments that require continuous adaptation.[165] When you approach execution with this kind of discipline, you reduce ambiguity, inspire confidence, and set a clear course forward.

When leaders can stay grounded in their strategy while taking decisive action, their choices tend to stay aligned with organizational values and vision. This creates a foundation for long-term success, empowering teams to contribute meaningfully to shared goals while maintaining adaptability to meet immediate demands. It's this alignment between big-picture strategy and day-to-day execution that strengthens organizations and makes them more resilient, focused, and ready to take on whatever challenges lie ahead. And let's face reality, for all the strategic analysis and planning that a leader does, there are still surprises during the execution phase.

---

[165] Finkelstein, S., Hambrick, D. C., & Cannella, A. A. (2009). *Strategic leadership: Theory and research on executives, top management teams, and boards*. Oxford University Press.

THE CHOICE MATRIX

The Choice Matrix is a decision-making compass that helps leaders navigate choices quickly and effectively, even amid the pressures of execution. By using the Choice Matrix, leaders can assess their options thoughtfully, ensuring their decision continue to align with core values and contributes to sustainable growth. It's not just about solving today's execution challenge; it's about making choices that build a stronger tomorrow.

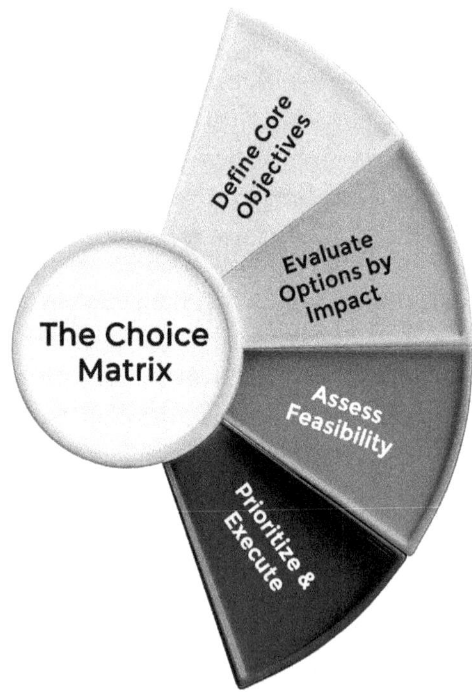

Here's how it works:

1. **Define What Matters Most**
   Every decision starts with clarity, even during a fast-paced execution. The first step in the Choice Matrix

is defining the core objectives driving the decision. What's the purpose behind this choice? How does it align with your organization's values and goals? Getting crystal clear about these objectives sets the foundation for everything else. This clarity not only reduces the risk of impulsive, off-track decisions, but also keeps your team aligned, ensuring everyone understands the *why* behind the actions you take.[166] It's guides everyone in the same direction.

2. **Weigh the Impact**

   Once your objectives are clear, it's time to evaluate how each option could play out. What's the immediate payoff? What's the long-term effect? Thinking through both short- and long-term impacts ensures you're not just reacting to the moment, but planning for the future. Research shows that leaders who focus on the broader picture are better equipped to steer their organizations through change and uncertainty.[167] This step pushes you to think about how each decision fits into the big picture, and ensures you're building resilience while addressing immediate needs. This is key during the execution phase.

3. **Ask: Is It Feasible?**

   Dreaming big is great, but execution is where the magic happens. So, it's important to ask, "Can this actually work?" "Do you have the resources?" "Is the timing

---

¹⁶⁶ Rumelt, R. (2011). *Good strategy, bad strategy: The difference and why it matters.* Crown Business.

¹⁶⁷ Eisenhardt, K. M., & Martin, J. A. (2000). Dynamic capabilities: What are they? *Strategic Management Journal, 21*(10-11), 1105–1121.
https://doi.org/10.1002/1097-0266(200010/11)21:10/11<1105:: AID-SMJ133>3.0.CO;2-E

right?" A feasibility check grounds your decisions and actions in reality, helping you recognize constraints and align your plans with what's achievable. Leaders who focus on feasibility are better prepared to execute their ideas effectively, avoiding overreach while staying ambitious.[168] This is where vision meets practicality, which is needed during the execution phase.

4. **Prioritize and Act**

    Finally, it's time to move forward. The Choice Matrix helps you narrow down your options to the ones that make the most sense strategically. Prioritizing the most impactful and feasible choices reduces decision fatigue and sets a clear path for action during the execution phase. Plus, when your team sees you moving forward with clarity, confidence, and purpose, it reinforces trust.

The beauty of the Choice Matrix is its ability to quickly turn complexity into action, which is exactly what you need during the execution phase. By defining your goals, evaluating impacts, checking feasibility, and prioritizing effectively, you create a process that takes the guesswork out of decision-making. It's a tool that doesn't just help you choose—it helps you lead. With the Choice Matrix, every decision becomes an opportunity to strengthen your organization's foundation, adapt to challenges, and stay aligned with your long-term vision.

KEY TAKEAWAYS

Execution with excellence is where vision becomes reality. The Atlantic Union Bank integration showed me that even the

---

[168] Levinthal, D. A., & March, J. G. (1993). The myopia of learning. *Strategic Management Journal, 14*(S2), 95–112. https://doi.org/10.1002/smj.4250141009

most talented teams cannot succeed without clarity, structure, and accountability. Everyone in that room wanted the same outcome, yet without defined priorities and ownership, we were paralyzed by competing voices and scattered effort. Once we reset the vision, established priorities, and assigned accountability, progress accelerated and excellence followed.

That is the power of this step in *the Juncture Code*. It's about execution rooted in alignment. Excellence does not come from doing everything; it comes from focusing on the right things, done in the right sequence, by the right people. It demands discipline to say no to distractions, courage to make hard choices, and humility to trust others to lead in their areas of responsibility.

Executing with excellence also builds confidence. Teams learn they can count on one another, leaders prove they can deliver, and organizations establish a reputation for reliability. This trust compounds, creating a culture where clarity, focus, and high standards are the norm. Over time, excellence becomes not just a practice, but an identity. Tools like the Choice Matrix make this possible.

As leaders, we must remember that execution is not about activity but about impact. It is not about speed alone but about precision and alignment. When strategy meets disciplined execution, organizations thrive. When we execute with excellence, we not only achieve our goals but also strengthen the very foundation of our leadership and our organizations for the challenges ahead.

1. **Strategic Decisions Balance Action and Vision**: Effective leadership requires aligning immediate actions with long-term goals. Leaders who combine strategic clarity with decisive execution create impactful out-

comes while ensuring their choices remain consistent with organizational values and the overall mission.[169]

2. **Structured Frameworks Enhance Confidence:** Tools like the Choice Matrix empower leaders to evaluate options thoroughly, balancing feasibility, impact, and alignment. This structured approach minimizes ambiguity, enabling leaders to act decisively in complex and dynamic environments.[170]

3. **Clarity Builds Trust:** Transparent, clear, and purposeful decision-making and execution foster trust and collaboration within teams. Leaders who communicate the rationale behind their choices amid the challenges of execution create alignment, empower innovation, and inspire collective ownership of organizational goals.

CASE STUDY: SHERYL SANDBERG'S STRATEGIC DECISIONS AND FACEBOOK'S GROWTH

Sheryl Sandberg's journey at Facebook, now Meta, is a masterclass in how focused, strategic decision-making and execution can drive explosive growth while keeping an organization resilient and adaptable. When Sandberg joined Facebook in 2008, the platform was at a critical juncture. It had the user base and momentum but needed a way to monetize the platform without upsetting the experience and losing the trust of loyal users. One of Sandberg's most impactful moves was her decision to introduce a data-driven advertising model. She saw Facebook's potential to revolutionize digital advertising by leveraging its

---

[169] Finkelstein, S., Hambrick, D. C., & Cannella, A. A. (2009). *Strategic leadership: Theory and research on executives, top management teams, and boards.* Oxford University Press.

[170] Thaler, R. H., & Sunstein, C. R. (2008). *Nudge: Improving decisions about health, wealth, and happiness.* Yale University Press.

vast troves of user data. Instead of guessing what might work, Sandberg and her team dug into the numbers, analyzing user behavior and industry trends to create highly targeted ads. This wasn't just a shot in the dark; it was a well-informed, strategic choice rooted in data. As Sandberg reflected, she relied on data to make decisions while remaining flexible enough to adapt to evolving user expectations and privacy concerns.[171] The results spoke for themselves. Facebook's advertising platform became a cornerstone of its revenue strategy, catapulting the company into one of the most valuable players in the advertising world.

What set Sandberg apart was her ability to balance profitability with a commitment to the user experience while executing on amid that tension. She understood that ads couldn't come at the expense of Facebook's core value of connection. By ensuring that advertisements complemented—rather than disrupted—the social experience, Sandberg helped maintain user trust and loyalty as the ad platform was introduced to the Facebook ecosystem. Her approach emphasized that strategic decisions shouldn't just aim for immediate results, they should also align with the organization's mission and a clear vision of long-term growth. This balancing act allowed Facebook to innovate without alienating its users, a lesson in how aligning choices with a mission can foster both growth and sustainability.

Adaptability was another hallmark of Sandberg's leadership. She recognized that sticking rigidly to a single plan could be risky, especially in a fast-moving industry. As mobile technology began to dominate, Sandberg pivoted Facebook's advertising model to prioritize mobile platforms. This wasn't just a minor tweak—it was a strategic shift that positioned

---

[171]   Sandberg, S. (2013). *Lean in: Women, work, and the will to lead.* Knopf.

Facebook to thrive in a rapidly evolving market. By focusing on mobile compatibility, Sandberg ensured that Facebook captured new audiences and stayed relevant. Her ability to pivot demonstrated the importance of blending long-term strategic vision with short-term responsiveness: a critical skill for leaders operating in dynamic environments.

Sandberg also prioritized transparency and collaboration within her team, creating a culture where everyone felt empowered to contribute. She encouraged open dialogue, ensuring that decisions were informed by diverse perspectives and aligned with Facebook's evolving goals. This approach reinforced a sense of shared purpose, making it easier for the organization to adapt to challenges.

As discussed already, the research by Amy C. Edmondson highlights the importance of psychological safety when it comes to encouraging innovation and resilience.[172] Sandberg modeled this approach, showing her team that even during the execution phase, clear, focused decision-making could be a shared effort rather than a top-down directive.

Sandberg's leadership at Facebook is a powerful example of how disciplined, data-driven decision-making, planning, and execution can shape an organization's trajectory. Her ability to align immediate goals with long-term vision, adapt to changing circumstances, and foster a collaborative culture provides invaluable lessons for leaders navigating their own strategic choices. Sandberg's story reminds us that great leadership is about more than making the right call; it's about making it with purpose, clarity, and adaptability.

----

[172] Edmondson, A. C. (2018). *The fearless organization: Creating psychological safety in the workplace for learning, innovation, and growth.* Wiley.

REFLECTION

Ask yourself the following questions and write your answers in your journal. After, take time to reflect on your discoveries.

1. How do you balance the need for timely action with the importance of thorough strategic analysis when making decisions?

2. What steps do you take to ensure your decisions align with both immediate priorities and long-term organizational objectives?

3. How do you evaluate the potential impacts, both short-term and long-term, of the options you consider?

4. In what ways do you foster collaboration and transparency within your team to support clear, focused decision-making?

5. What strategies can you implement to remain adaptable and responsive without compromising your core values or vision?

SELF-AUDIT

Rate yourself on a scale from one to ten, where one means "rarely or not at all" and ten means "frequently or very well."

1. I make strategic decisions that balance immediate priorities with long-term objectives.

   1   2   3   4   5   6   7   8   9   10

2. I utilize a structured approach to evaluate options before committing to a course of action.

   1   2   3   4   5   6   7   8   9   10

3. I ensure my decisions align with the mission, vision, and values of the organization.

| 1 | 2 | 3 | 4 | 5 | 6 | 7 | 8 | 9 | 10 |

4. I effectively communicate the rationale behind my decisions to foster team alignment.

| 1 | 2 | 3 | 4 | 5 | 6 | 7 | 8 | 9 | 10 |

5. I remain open to revising my decisions based on new insights or evolving circumstances.

| 1 | 2 | 3 | 4 | 5 | 6 | 7 | 8 | 9 | 10 |

6. I incorporate both risks and rewards into my decision-making process to ensure balance.

| 1 | 2 | 3 | 4 | 5 | 6 | 7 | 8 | 9 | 10 |

7. I actively seek input from diverse perspectives to refine my strategic choices.

| 1 | 2 | 3 | 4 | 5 | 6 | 7 | 8 | 9 | 10 |

8. I reflect on the outcomes of previous decisions to enhance my future decision-making practices.

| 1 | 2 | 3 | 4 | 5 | 6 | 7 | 8 | 9 | 10 |

9. I prioritize decisions that advance both immediate outcomes and sustainable growth.

| 1 | 2 | 3 | 4 | 5 | 6 | 7 | 8 | 9 | 10 |

10. I balance decisiveness with adaptability, adjusting my course when necessary while staying true to core goals.

| 1 | 2 | 3 | 4 | 5 | 6 | 7 | 8 | 9 | 10 |

Identify a significant decision or challenge you're currently facing and use the following steps to develop a clear and actionable plan:

1. **Define the Decision Context:** Start by outlining the specific situation and its importance. What is at stake? What are the immediate needs and long-term goals associated with this decision?

2. **Set Clear Objectives**: Articulate the primary objectives guiding your decision. Make sure these objectives align with your organization's mission, vision, and values. Reflect on how success would be defined for this decision.

3. **Generate and Evaluate Options:** Brainstorm at least three possible approaches to address the decision. Evaluate each option for:

   - Feasibility: Does your team have the necessary resources and capabilities?

   - Impact: How will this option influence immediate results and long-term strategy?

   - Alignment: Does it support organizational goals and reflect core values?

4. **Prioritize and Decide:** Based on your evaluation, rank the options. Identify the top choice and create a backup plan in case adjustments are required. Write down the rationale behind your selected option to reinforce clarity and purpose.

5. **Plan for Execution:** Develop an actionable roadmap to implement your decision. Identify key milestones, resource needs, and potential risks. Ensure your team is aligned with the plan and understands their roles.

6. **Reflect and Adapt:** Schedule a checkpoint after executing your decision to evaluate its progress and outcomes. Consider: What is working? What needs adjustment? How can this experience inform future decision-making?

This exercise ensures that your decisions are not only strategic, but actionable. It integrates clarity, alignment, and adaptability, empowering you to lead with confidence and purpose while remaining responsive to evolving circumstances.

CHAPTER 15

LEARN FROM OUTCOMES

"Reflect on your strengths and use them as your base."

—Angela Duckworth

ONE OF THE most transformative experiences of my leadership journey came when I was tasked with expanding my district while at PaineWebber in the early 1990s. The investment was significant, the stakes were high, the timeline was aggressive, and the expectations were immense. This wasn't just about achieving financial targets; it was about building two new offices from the ground up while inspiring a team that was still finding its rhythm. Early on, it seemed we were on track. The initial work hit most of the milestones, and the team's energy was growing. But as we moved past the first phase, cracks in our plans began to show: a build-out delay, hiring miscues, equipment backlogs, and operational bottlenecks. Team morale wavered. I could feel the weight of every missed target, and knew we needed to consider a new direction—but where to begin?

I remember sitting down for lunch one day, poring over reports and timelines and trying to identify where we'd gone wrong. It was easy to get lost in a blame game, but then I thought, *What if the answers aren't just in the data? What if they are in how we've approached the process?* I shifted my focus. Instead of hunting for mistakes, I started asking myself more questions: *What assumptions are we making about our clients? How are team dynamics influencing execution? Are we measuring the right things to define success?*

The next day, I gathered the leadership team and shared my revelations. Together, we dissected our decisions and discussed our challenges. What emerged was a pattern of well-intentioned but flawed assumptions. We had overestimated delivery times and underestimated the complexity of some workflows. More importantly, we hadn't built enough feedback loops into our process to catch these issues earlier. Our analysis of the situation changed everything. We didn't just adjust our strategy—we redefined how we worked as a team. We built checkpoints into every phase of the project, established weekly meetings for candid feedback, and made reflection an integral part of our team culture. Over the following months, not only did we recover from our initial missteps, but we exceeded our original goals.

Looking back, this experience wasn't just about solving a particular challenge; it was about learning a foundational truth about leadership. Success isn't only about moving forward—it's about pausing to look back and learn from the journey so you can move forward more effectively. This step in the Juncture Code is about learning from outcomes and

     DAVID L ZIMMERMAN, MSC, CPC

turning every experience into an opportunity for professional development and growth. Reflection allows leaders to step back, evaluate what worked and what didn't, and adapt their strategies with greater insight and precision. Leadership is filled with twists, turns, and unexpected challenges. American academic, psychologist, and popular science author Angela Duckworth's groundbreaking book, *Grit: The Power of Passion and Perseverance* reminds us that critical success traits are magnified by thoughtful reflection.[173] Leaders who commit to learning from their outcomes develop a level of resilience that prepares them for the complexities of modern leadership. In this chapter we'll move beyond surface-level analysis into a deeper exploration of the patterns, assumptions, and beliefs that drive decision-making, and how analyzing these drivers can turn reflection into a powerful tool for leaders and teams to develop resilience, adaptability, and sustainable success.

GRIT, RESILIENCE, AND REFLECTIVE GROWTH

When resilience and reflective growth come together, they create a powerful cycle of continuous learning and improvement. The ability to bounce back and grow stronger after setbacks, to be resilient, is also key, and depends on leaders' ability to reflect on their outcomes, adjust course, and learn from their experiences. Teresa Amabile and Steven Kramer, in their work on what they call the "Progress Principle," propose that leaders who embrace this mindset are more adaptable and better equipped to thrive in the long run, as they are constantly refining their strategies to keep up with the changing landscape.[174] It's not about glossing over failures or setbacks,

---

[173]   Duckworth, A. (2016). *Grit: The power of passion and perseverance*. Scribner.

[174]   Amabile, T. M., & Kramer, S. J. (2011). *The progress principle: Using small wins to ignite joy, engagement, and creativity at work*. Harvard Business Review Press.

but digging into them to find the lessons within and then adapting accordingly. This reflective approach doesn't just solve immediate problems; it builds a foundation for future growth and sustained adaptability.

Going a layer deeper, reflection becomes even more powerful when it's intentional and structured. Chris Argyris, known for his seminal work on learning organizations, and Donald Schon, who developed the reflective practice in business, worked together on the concept of double-loop learning, which challenges leaders to go beyond surface-level fixes and explore the deeper beliefs and assumptions driving their decisions.[175] For example, if a project goes off course, instead of just asking, "What went wrong?" double-loop learning pushes leaders to ask, "What assumptions led us to this decision?" This deeper reflection helps leaders address root causes, which ultimately leads to smarter, more sustainable strategies moving forward. Ross Thornley, CEO and Co-Founder of AQai an adaptability assessments business, developed the concept of an adaptability intelligence (AQ), which adds yet another dimension to this conversation. Thornley emphasizes that grit and reflective growth are key drivers of AQ, the ability to adapt and thrive in the face of change.[176] Leaders with a high AQ don't just weather storms—they learn how to adjust their sails mid-journey and use them to their advantage. These leaders create teams and organizations that are not only resilient, but also adaptive and innovative, ready to pivot when the unexpected happens. By weaving reflective growth into their leadership approach, they build a culture where learning and agility become second nature.

---

[175] Argyris, C., & Schon, D. A. (1978). *Organizational learning: A theory of action perspective.* Addison-Wesley.

[176] Thornley, R. (2020). *Decoding AQ: Adaptability Intelligence for Successful Leaders.* Adaptai Press.

Peter Senge of MIT expands on this idea by showing how reflective growth can shape an entire organization. In a true "learning organization," reflection isn't limited to the individual leader—it's a shared practice that empowers teams to adapt collectively.[177] When leaders prioritize learning and resilience, they create an environment where people feel safe to take risks, learn from their mistakes, and bring fresh ideas to the table. This kind of culture doesn't just respond to change—it anticipates it, making the organization stronger and more cohesive. Ultimately, grit, resilience, and reflective growth are deeply interconnected. Leaders who embody these traits don't just adapt to their environments, they shape them. This creates a ripple effect, fostering a culture of continuous growth and innovation that positions both leaders and their organizations to thrive in an ever-changing world.

THE OUTCOME REFLECTION MODEL

The Outcome Reflection Model, often associated with Gibbs' Reflective Cycle, is one of the best frameworks I know in terms of fostering resilience and growth. It is a structured approach to learning from experience. It involves analyzing past events to understand what happened, why, and how to improve future actions. The model typically includes stages: describing the experience; reflecting on feelings; evaluating the situation; analyzing the cause; concluding with lessons learned; and outlining an action plan for future scenarios.[178]

The Outcome Reflection Model offers a practical and intentional way for leaders to evaluate the outcomes of their decisions, transforming those experiences into meaningful

---

[177]   Senge, P. M. (2006). *The fifth discipline: The art and practice of the learning organization.* Crown Business.

[178]   We need a citation for this reference.

growth opportunities. Think of it as a structured roadmap for reflecting on what worked, what didn't, and, most importantly, what you can do better next time. By taking a disciplined approach to reflection, leaders can uncover insights that improve not only their decision-making but also their ability to adapt and thrive in future challenges. Here's how the Outcome Reflection Model works:

1. **Identify Decision and Intended Goals**
   Start by revisiting the decision you made and the goals you were aiming for. What were you trying to achieve? Getting crystal clear on your original intentions gives you a strong foundation for evaluating what happened. It's not just about knowing the *what*—it's about under-standing the *why* behind your choices.

2. **Evaluate Results**
   Now take a close look at the actual outcomes. Did they align with your goals? What worked well? What didn't? This isn't about assigning blame—it's about learning. By comparing your intended outcomes with the actual results, you can start to uncover patterns and trends that will be useful moving forward.

3. **Analyze Contributing Factors**
   Every outcome has its backstory. Was there something about your team's dynamics, available resources, or external challenges that played a role? Maybe there was a shift in priorities or unexpected obstacles. By identifying the factors that influenced your results, you gain a better understanding of what's within your control and what's not.

4. **Extract Key Learnings**

    This is where the real growth happens. What specific lessons can you take away from this experience? What should you repeat? What should you do differently next time? Reflect on both your successes and your challenges—there's value in both. The goal here is to build a personal "playbook" of insights you can draw on in future decisions.

5. **Plan for Future Application**

    Reflection without action doesn't get you very far. The final step is to take what you've learned and apply it to your next challenge. How will these insights shape your future decisions? By setting clear intentions for how you'll use what you've learned, you ensure that reflection leads to growth, not just understanding.

OUTCOME REFLECTION MODEL YES

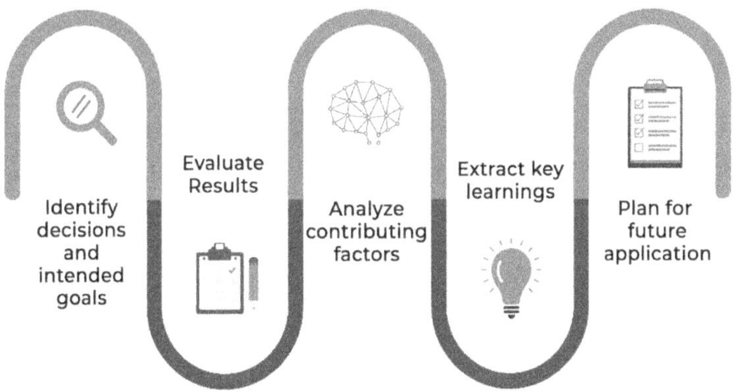

The beauty of the Outcome Reflection Model is its simplicity and focus on actionable insights. It's not about getting stuck in endless analysis or overthinking past decisions. Instead, it's about using every experience; good, bad, or somewhere in between as an opportunity to refine your approach. When you build this practice into your leadership routines, it becomes a powerful tool for continuous improvement, helping you make more intentional, informed decisions over time. As you apply these insights to future challenges, you'll find that each decision, no matter the outcome, adds to your capacity to lead with resilience, adaptability, and purpose.

KEY TAKEAWAYS

My experience at PaineWebber taught me that leadership is not about flawless execution or the absence of setbacks, it's about what we choose to do with the outcomes we create. I learned that progress doesn't come from chasing perfection, but from pausing, reflecting, and recalibrating. The real turning point wasn't when we finally hit our targets—it was when we stopped trying to simply "fix" problems and instead started asking deeper questions about our assumptions, processes, and shared beliefs.

As Angela Duckworth reminds us, reflection strengthens grit. Grit without reflection risks becoming blind persistence, but when paired with resilience and intentional learning, it becomes a force for growth. And significant research underscores this truth. Leaders who examine not only *what* happened, but *why* it happened develop the insight to lead more adaptively. When companies become learning organizations, they can take this even further, transforming into agile, forward-looking operations.

Finally, the Outcome Reflection Model offers us a way to make this practice tangible. By systematically examining decisions, results, and assumptions, and then applying lessons forward, leaders ensure that no experience, whether success or failure, is wasted. This is the essence of the Juncture Code: turning

    DAVID L ZIMMERMAN, MSC, CPC

outcomes into opportunities, setbacks into steppingstones, and reflection into resilience. Leadership is a journey, and reflection is the compass that keeps us moving forward in the right direction with clarity, adaptability, and purpose.

1. **Reflection Drives Resilience and Adaptability:** Reflective practices allow leaders to transform both successes and setbacks into valuable learning opportunities. This approach enhances resilience by fostering a mindset focused on growth, adaptability, and continuous improvement.

2. **The Outcome Reflection Model as a Practical Framework:** The structured approach of the Outcome Reflection Model helps leaders systematically evaluate decisions, uncover root causes, and align future actions with organizational goals. This method ensures reflection translates into actionable insights and long-term growth.

3. **Embedding Reflective Growth in Organizational Culture:** Leaders who prioritize reflection and encourage open discussions about outcomes inspire a culture of learning and resilience. This collaborative approach equips teams to navigate uncertainty with confidence, fostering innovation and shared accountability.

CASE STUDY: HOW ED CATMULL BUILT A CULTURE OF REFLECTION AT PIXAR

When Ed Catmull helped launch Pixar, he had one goal: to create the first full-length computer-animated film. That dream became reality in 1995 with *Toy Story*, a groundbreaking success that changed animation forever. But behind the triumph was a growing concern. The Pixar team was brilliant, full of creative geniuses and technical pioneers, but as the company scaled, Catmull began to see a dangerous pattern emerging. People were starting to believe their own hype. Success was becoming a shield that prevented honest reflection. Catmull recognized this as a form of organizational bias: the success trap. It's the subtle belief that if something worked before, it would keep working to the future. He realized that Pixar's greatest threat wasn't a failure, but complacency. So, he made a counterintuitive decision: he institutionalized learning from failure.

Under Catmull's leadership, Pixar built systems that encouraged candid reflection after every project. One of the most powerful reflection tools he introduced was the "postmortem," which was a structured, company-wide review where directors, artists, and engineers examined what went right, what went wrong, and what could be done better next time. These sessions weren't about blame—they were about unearthing valuable insight. Catmull often reminded his teams, "Mistakes aren't a necessary evil. They're the inevitable consequence of doing something new."[179] This mindset reframed failure as an opportunity to grow, learn, and improve.

At one point, during the early production of *Toy Story 2*, Pixar nearly lost the entire film due to a technical glitch that deleted months of work. A single line of errant code had wiped the servers clean. The catastrophe could have been fatal—but rather than searching for someone to blame, Catmull and his leadership team chose to reflect. They examined their assumptions about system backups and communication. The result was a complete overhaul of Pixar's infrastructure

---

[179] Catmull, E., & Wallace, A. (2014). *Creativity, Inc.: Overcoming the unseen forces that stand in the way of true inspiration*. Random House.

and workflow—a change that not only saved the project, but ultimately made Pixar stronger.[180]

Catmull's disciplined inclusion of reflection helped Pixar achieve a nearly unprecedented record of critical and commercial successes, each built on lessons from the last. Catmull later wrote, "We made the decision early on that we would not hide our failures. We'd use them to teach ourselves how to be better."[181] That statement captures the essence of learning from outcomes, transforming experience into intelligence, and mistakes into momentum.

Ed Catmull's legacy at Pixar stands as a masterclass in reflective leadership. His willingness to confront the biases of success, embrace vulnerability, and create psychological safety for honest dialogue allowed the organization to grow, innovate, and adapt. His story reminds us that progress doesn't come from avoiding mistakes, it comes from mining them for wisdom.

REFLECTION

Ask yourself the following questions and write your answers in your journal. After, take time to reflect on your discoveries.

1. How do you approach reflecting on both successes and setbacks, and what patterns emerge in your decision-making process?

---

[180] Owen, L. (2022, February 15). How *"Toy Story 2" got deleted twice, once on accident, again for its own good*. The Next Web. *https://www.thenextweb.com/news/how-pixars-toy-story-2-was-deleted-twice-once-by-technology-and-again-for-its-own-good*

[181] 4BIS. (2025, November 13). *How "Toy Story 2" was almost deleted: Data loss lessons*. 4BIS. *https://www.4bis.com/toy-story-data-loss/*

2. What practices do you use to ensure lessons learned from past outcomes are applied to future decisions?

3. How do you challenge the assumptions behind decisions that didn't yield the expected results?

4. In what ways can you support your team in viewing mistakes as opportunities for growth rather than setbacks?

5. How do you integrate resilience and adaptability into your decision-making framework to better handle uncertainty?

SELF-AUDIT

Rate yourself on a scale from one to ten, where one means "rarely or not at all" and ten means "frequently or very well."

1. I consistently reflect on both the successes and challenges of my decisions.

1	2	3	4	5	6	7	8	9	10

2. I actively seek to uncover and challenge assumptions underlying my decisions.

1	2	3	4	5	6	7	8	9	10

3. I integrate lessons learned from past outcomes into my future strategies.

1	2	3	4	5	6	7	8	9	10

4. I create opportunities for my team to reflect on their experiences and grow from them.

1	2	3	4	5	6	7	8	9	10

5. I view setbacks as opportunities to build resilience and adaptability.

   1   2   3   4   5   6   7   8   9   10

6. I value structured reflection as a cornerstone of my leadership effectiveness.

   1   2   3   4   5   6   7   8   9   10

7. I encourage open discussions about outcomes to promote learning within my team.

   1   2   3   4   5   6   7   8   9   10

8. I use feedback as a tool to refine my decision-making and leadership approach.

   1   2   3   4   5   6   7   8   9   10

9. I remain adaptable, recalibrating my strategies based on new information and outcomes.

   1   2   3   4   5   6   7   8   9   10

10. I model resilience and a learning mindset for my team, inspiring them to embrace challenges.

   1   2   3   4   5   6   7   8   9   10

EXERCISE: RESILIENCE THROUGH REFLECTION

1. **Select a Decision to Reflect On**
   Choose a recent significant decision, whether it led to success, a challenge, or unexpected results.

2. **Define the Decision Context**
   Write down the decision's context, including:

   o   The objectives you aimed to achieve.

   o   The factors or circumstances influencing the decision.

3. **Evaluate the Outcome**
   Analyze the results by asking:

   o   What went well? What exceeded expectations?

   o   What fell short, and why?

4. **Identify Contributing Factors**
   Reflect on the factors that shaped the outcome:

   o   Were there internal influences, such as team dynamics or assumptions, that played a role?

   o   Were there external influences, such as market shifts or unforeseen challenges?

5. **Extract Key Learnings**
   Document the lessons learned:

   o   How did this experience improve your understanding of decision-making?

   o   What new insights did you gain about resilience, adaptability, or leadership?

6. **Plan for Application**
   Set three specific intentions for applying these lessons to future decisions:

   o   What will you do differently next time?

   o   How will you involve your team in reflective practices to strengthen collective resilience?

7. **Collaborate with Your Team (Optional)**
   Share your findings with your team, encouraging open
   discussion about the decision and what everyone can
   learn from it. Foster a culture of shared growth and
   adaptability.

CHAPTER 16

YOUR PERSONAL JUNCTURE CODE

*"When you create the process, you ignite a sense of
ownership that fuels the will to overcome obstacles"*

—David Zimmerman

WHEN I ENTERED the brokerage business in the 1980s,
the industry was much like the one portrayed in *The
Wolf of Wall Street*. It was driven by a hard-sell, take-no-prisoners
approach, where daily, weekly, and monthly commissions often
mattered more than the clients themselves. For many brokers,
success was measured solely by short-term gains, not by the
quality of relationships built—but this didn't align with my
values or approach to business.

Armed with a Certified Financial Planner (CFP) designation and
five years of family office experience at a private trust company
where I gained both financial planning and managed advisory
services experience, I envisioned a client-centered model that

emphasized trust, respect, and long-term financial wellness. I introduced a model that prioritized comprehensive financial planning and managed money solutions over transactional sales. I focused on understanding each client's unique needs, goals, and challenges before making any recommendations.

This required a shift in mindset for my clients and my team. Rather than pushing products, I fostered conversations around financial goals and strategies. Clients responded positively, valuing the time and depth of insight, which in turn built a foundation of loyalty and trust. But this approach was not initially well received. Colleagues, and even my manager, questioned my methods, and I frequently had to defend the long-term value of client-centered practices against the prevailing drive for short-term sales goals. I had to learn to stand my ground and defend my decisions. In the end, my approach paid off and enabled me to generate over $400,000 in annual recurring revenue by my third year in the business.

Pioneering this model, and taking the risk to stand out, led me into the Shearson Lehman Hutton management training program. Three years later, I was asked to move to New York to fill a newly-created position as Head of Advanced Financial Advisor (FA) Development. My confidence and ability to deliver had propelled me into leadership. But, boy, did I have my moments of self-doubt. I wish I'd known then what I know now. The Juncture Code would have been a lifesaver back in those early days of my career.

In many ways, this part of my journey became the foundation of my leadership philosophy and a testament to the power of intentional change. Shifting the focus from quick sales to client-centered financial management wasn't just a new approach for the times—it was an exercise in applying resilience, adaptability, and a disciplined commitment to my values. This evolution—from pushing products to establishing a structured, client-centered practice—underscored the principles embedded in the Juncture Code, like self-awareness, strategic analysis and planning, checking for biases, and learning from outcomes. My professional experiences continued to reinforce the importance of each of these steps. Today, as I continue to champion these principles, I'm reminded how important it is to equip leaders with tools and structures to help them navigate pivotal moments with confidence. It's why I wrote The Juncture Code and why this last part of the book is about making the code your own.

The journey through The Juncture Code thus far, has been about exposing leaders like you to a robust foundation for resilient, adaptive, and intentional decision-making in the face of continuous change and challenges. Each step introduced new tools and structures designed to help attain more clarity, focus on the right things, create stability while navigating key junctures, and learn from the entire experience. Yet, for leaders who seek transformative and lasting impact, the Juncture Code offers an additional dimension: personalization. While the structured code lays the groundwork, tailoring each step to your unique personal goals and leadership style will enable you to unlock the Code's full potential and create a model uniquely aligned with your commitments, experiences, and aspirations. Now, the Juncture Code can become a deeply personalized compass. Customization also allows for a dynamic, evolving structure that can be adjusted as you grow in your role as a leader, ensuring that decisions reflect both a commitment to personal principles and a strategic approach to challenges. Research supports that leaders who create action plans based on intrinsic values and personal priorities experience greater engagement, satisfaction, and sustained influence.[182]

---

[182]   Bennis, W. (2009). *On becoming a leader*. Basic Books.

   DAVID L ZIMMERMAN, MSC, CPC

So, let's explore how to transform the Juncture Code into a highly specific, actionable plan, unique to your journey and authentic identity.

YOUR JOURNEY, YOUR CODE

Customization in leadership isn't about reinventing the wheel—it's about ensuring that the tools you use reflect the distinct terrain of your personal journey. Leadership is deeply intertwined with your values, beliefs, and experiences. Customization allows you to adapt the guidance and structures shared in these pages and turn them into your own unique roadmap. This step is about creation and ownership. When leaders craft their own personal code, they're not blindly following the steps of a certain process—they're building and adapting a system that grows with them. By tailoring each phase of the Juncture Code to their priorities, leaders enhance focus and deepen their commitment to their decisions and the work to be done. This personalization doesn't just strengthen individual effectiveness; it radiates outward, shaping team dynamics and organizational culture.

Customization is also fluid. Leaders and leadership challenges evolve, and so should your approach. As your career progresses, your personal Juncture Code should shift to stay in sync with you and the world around you. That's why revisiting and refining your customized code will help you stay agile, current, and forward looking. Personalization of the Juncture Code is really about a mindset shift. It encourages you to see your personal and professional growth as a process of intentional design, rather than something you just learn in a book. It becomes *yours*. Ultimately, customization ensures that the Juncture Code is not just a guide, but a living, breathing expression of your unique values, beliefs, experiences, talents, and authentic identity as a leader. It transforms decision-making, as well as navigating challenges and change, into a personal art form, where every step is infused with your own passion, priorities, and purpose. So, let's look at the six steps of the Juncture Code in a new, more personal light:

- Develop self-awareness.

- Take a strategic approach.

- Challenge assumptions and biases.

- Execute with excellence.

- Learn from outcomes.

A MORE SELF-AWARE YOU

As we have discussed at length, deeply understanding yourself, your values, biases, and motivations is crucial if you want to approach decisions and challenges with integrity and authenticity. So, how do you make this step in the Juncture Code your own? How does this foundational step become part of your unique leadership style? What are you willing to do to become a more self-aware leader? It's time for you to make a personal commitment. List out specific, actionable goals for personal growth in this area. Examples of steps to deepen self-awareness could include:

Semi-Annual 360-Degree Feedback Sessions: regular feedback from colleagues, direct reports, and supervisors, which can help identify blind spots and strengths.

Personal Reflection and Journaling: a daily or weekly journal where you reflect on your decisions, challenges, and emotions, helping you track your growth over time.

Leadership Coaching: bi-weekly coaching sessions that offer guided self-reflection and skill-building from a trained professional.

Self-Assessment Tools and Tests: invest in quarterly assessments—like REACHlx, AQme or Clifton Strengths—that will provide insights into personality traits and preferences.

Personal Values Statement: draft a statement outlining your core values and revisit it regularly—especially when faced with tough decision-making.

WHAT WILL YOUR STRATEGIC APPROACH BE?

We've discussed the concrete value of strategic analysis and planning. The benefits of this approach are bigger than you as a leader. So, how do you own the strategic process as a leader? How do you make this part of the DNA of your leadership style? You can't leave it to chance; you need to operationalize it as part of your daily way of doing business. But what does that look like? To start, you need to align your strategic analysis and planning with your priorities. Define the methods and metrics that are most relevant to your long-term objectives as a leader. Examples of personalized action steps for strategic analysis and planning might include:

Reviews with Mentors: regularly engaging in guided analysis sessions with industry mentors to help maintain your focus on evolving industry standards and trends.

Customer Feedback Analysis: regularly reviewing customer feedback data to identify potential shifts in client expectations and to operationalize your strategic approach.

Competitor Benchmarking: conducting a bi-annual competitor analysis to compare and gain insight on strategic positioning—giving you the strategic data you need to stay competitive.

Future-Focused Workshops: regularly scheduling brainstorming sessions with trusted advisors who are willing to challenge current strategies and examine future possibilities as a means of staying at the front of the pack.[183]

Personal Development Goals: reviewing your personal development goals alongside your strategic goals to ensure that your decisions are holistically aligned.

HOW WILL YOU CHALLENGE ASSUMPTIONS AND BIASES?

As a leader, you know you have to question preconceived notions and habitual thinking. Leaders who challenge assumptions foster innovation by exploring alternative perspectives: sparking creativity and innovation. So, what practices can you adopt to promote balanced decision-making? Here are some ideas:

Diverse Brainstorming Sessions: invite monthly feedback from teams outside of your usual circles,

---

[183] Drucker, P. F. (2008). *The essential Drucker: The best of sixty years of Peter Drucker's essential writings on management.* Harper Business.

including colleagues from other departments or industries; be sure to put these sessions on the calendar and mark them as a priority.

Assumption Reviews: regular discussions with trusted peers to assess and evaluate assumptions behind current decisions to empower your people and become a more informed and aware leader.

Bias Workshops: attend workshops on an ongoing basis about cognitive biases. This is how to stay informed on how biases can influence decision-making. This is an important form of professional development for you and your team.

Devil's Advocate Sessions: appoint a team member to challenge your strategic analysis and plans with alternative perspectives; try to do this monthly.

Decision Log: maintain a log of your major decisions, noting initial assumptions, actions, and outcomes to identify recurring biases. You can journal after each log entry to capture key learnings.

HOW WILL YOU EXPAND YOUR OPTIONS?

As you generate a range of actionable alternatives in preparation to face change or a challenge, it's important to make sure to encourage creative and expansive thinking. As we have discussed, this approach has numerous benefits for you and your team, so make sure it's part of your approach to leadership. You can customize this step of the Juncture Code by incorporating specific habits into your schedule in order to inspire innovative thinking and decision-making. Possible steps include:

Cross-Disciplinary Meetings: Consider bringing in experts at least twice a year from different fields to brainstorm fresh approaches to challenges.

Innovation Luncheons: Try setting up informal monthly brainstorming luncheons that focus on creative problem-solving and comradery.

Idea Incubators: Dedicate regularly scheduled time and resources to help you and your team develop unconventional ideas and explore what-if scenarios in a more structured way—and not only when you need to respond to something. This is about creating a culture of innovation.

Pain-Point Reviews: If you want to make the Juncture Code your own, you need to look at the good, the bad, and the ugly. Regularly scheduled sessions to review pain points and unique solutions to them will ensure that you and your team don't skip the hard stuff.

Blue Sky Sessions: Conversely, brainstorm without fear of judgement or constraint should be a regular and ongoing practice for you and your team. It will encourage everyone to think outside the box and foster unconventional options. Again, this is as much about building a creative culture as fostering specific ideas. The practice will far exceed the ideas generated at any single meeting.

HOW WILL YOU EXECUTE WITH EXCELLENCE?

When you take a strategic approach to decision-making and navigating change, it's much easier to execute with excellence. However, you have your own style on execution and implementation, so this step of the Juncture Code deserves personalization, too. How will you balance short-term needs with long-term goals when you're executing fast? What does that look like for you and your team? How will you stay grounded, adaptable, and effective amid the heightened pressure? You need to define a style for implementing decisions that reflects your authentic approach to leadership. Examples of action steps for choice execution include:

> **Feedback Loops:** Schedule regular feedback sessions after implementing a decision to monitor progress and adjust if necessary. Set the ground rules so everyone feels heard and respected in these sessions.

> **Detailed Roadmaps:** For each major decision, draft a clear action plan that outlines responsibilities, timelines, and milestones. What level of detail makes you and your team feel comfortable and empowered? Make sure your roadmaps includes how to handle roadblocks and other surprises, which are inevitable when you and your team are executing your business plan.

> **Delegated Authority:** If empowerment is a priority for you as a leader, create a delegation structure that entrusts team members to implement key aspects of any given project or goal. This might end up being a key characteristic of your leadership style and one that engenders significant trust and respect.

> **Execution Check Ins:** Alignment is key during execution. To keep teams aligned, consider holding regular check-ins to track progress and address

any roadblocks. This shows that you want to hear from your team and respect their input and ideas.

Accountability Partner: Select a peer to regularly check in on your leadership during the execution phase. Incorporating an accountability partner will keep you on track and ensure consistent execution and follow-through.

WHAT'S THE BEST WAY TO LEARN FROM YOUR OUTCOMES?

Reflecting on your results as a leader helps you identify lessons and areas for personal and team growth. One individualized tool I like to use with my clients is the Outcome Reflection Model, which integrates methods that support deep personal growth. Reflection-focused action steps might include:

Peer Review: You'll notice that peer review is a step we've mentioned before. Meeting with peers to discuss recent outcomes, progress toward strategic goals, and key lessons is a great way to create a learning culture.

Journaling: This is another tool we've mentioned before, and perhaps it's the most customizable of all. As long as your writing down your thoughts about major decisions on a regular basis, you'll see the benefits of journaling in many aspects of your leadership over time. It's very powerful.

Feedback Surveys: Gathering feedback through regularly scheduled surveys is a great way to gather insights from team members on decisions that impact them and to gain varied perspectives.

Self-Reflection Exercises: This is a great way to reinforce your efforts to become more self-aware. You can work on self-awareness preemptively, but also retroactively, taking time to self-reflect after major decisions have been executed. It's a different way to assess your self-awareness after the fact—and consider areas for continued personal development and growth.

Debriefs: You can take these exercises a bit farther by making them a group effort. After each major project, hold debriefing sessions with your to collectively review and reflect upon what worked and what didn't.

LOOKING TOWARD THE FUTURE GUIDED BY YOUR CODE

By defining and committing to specific actions within each step, you have created a unique personal model that aligns with your individual journey, enabling the Juncture Code to function as both a structured guide and an authentic expression of your vision. Every principle we've explored together, reflection and self-audit you've undertaken, and each exercise you've done has been designed to provide a structure to help you face the inevitable challenges and change that confront leaders every day. The journey here has not been merely one of theory, but of personal transformation. This isn't a conclusion, but a beginning, where the Juncture Code can now become a living, breathing part of how you approach every significant decision and crossroads as a leader. At its core, leadership is a commitment to ongoing growth and alignment. It's a responsibility that requires you to remain anchored in who you are and what you stand for, even as the demands of the world shift beneath your feet. The Juncture Code doesn't ask you to adhere to a fixed formula, instead, it provides a reliable foundation that can be revisited, revised, and reinvigorated over time. Through self-awareness, strategic analysis and planning, challenging your assumptions and biases, executing with excellence, and learning from outcomes, these practices and structures are meant to be a guiding compass on your leadership journey. But the true power of the Juncture Code lies in its renewability. The flexible nature of this code allows you to adjust and refine it as you evolve both personally and professionally. Through each of its pillars, the Juncture Code enables you to cultivate a leadership style grounded in your unique values, beliefs, and experiences, positioning you to lead from a place of authenticity and strength for the length of your career and beyond.

REFLECTION

Here's a list that dives into self-reflection for crafting a unique Personal Code:

1. How will I prioritize consistency and commitment to my chosen action steps?

2. What practices can I implement to regularly review and refine my personal Code?

3. How will I measure success or progress within each customized step?

4. What will I do if I encounter resistance (internally or externally) in implementing my personal Code?

5. How can I ensure that each step in my personal Code remains relevant as my career evolves?

6. What feedback mechanisms can I set up to continuously improve my personal Code?

7. How can I effectively communicate my customized approach to others?

8. In what ways will my personal version of the code encourage learning and adaptation?

9. How can I ensure that this personalized approach empowers my decision-making at every juncture?

10. What will I do if my personal Code feels misaligned with organizational goals?

SELF-AUDIT

Rate yourself on a scale from one to ten, where one means "rarely or not at all" and ten means "frequently or very well."

1. I have clearly defined my core values and principles.

    1   2   3   4   5   6   7   8   9   10

2. I feel confident in identifying specific actions for each step of the Juncture Code.

    1   2   3   4   5   6   7   8   9   10

3. I am open to adjusting my framework as I grow and encounter new challenges.

    1   2   3   4   5   6   7   8   9   10

4. I know which self-awareness practices will enhance my leadership.

    1   2   3   4   5   6   7   8   9   10

5. My personalized approach encourages a collaborative, resilient team culture.

    1   2   3   4   5   6   7   8   9   10

6. I regularly check that my customized steps align with my broader objectives.

| 1 | 2 | 3 | 4 | 5 | 6 | 7 | 8 | 9 | 10 |

7. I am committed to refining my approach based on real-world feedback.

| 1 | 2 | 3 | 4 | 5 | 6 | 7 | 8 | 9 | 10 |

8. I prioritize resilience and adaptability in my decision-making process.

| 1 | 2 | 3 | 4 | 5 | 6 | 7 | 8 | 9 | 10 |

9. I maintain alignment between my personal Code and organizational goals.

| 1 | 2 | 3 | 4 | 5 | 6 | 7 | 8 | 9 | 10 |

10. I recognize the importance of evolving my framework over time.

| 1 | 2 | 3 | 4 | 5 | 6 | 7 | 8 | 9 | 10 |

11. I have built-in accountability for adhering to my personal Code.

| 1 | 2 | 3 | 4 | 5 | 6 | 7 | 8 | 9 | 10 |

12. I feel that my personal Code is a true reflection of my unique leadership path.

| 1 | 2 | 3 | 4 | 5 | 6 | 7 | 8 | 9 | 10 |

FINAL THOUGHTS

If we were sitting across from each other right now, as you finish reading The Juncture Code, I would say thank you for trusting me to walk beside you. You didn't have to stick with it to the end. You could have skimmed the stories, nodded at the research, and moved on. Instead, you stayed and wrestled with the hard questions about your thinking, stress, biases, identity, relationships, and what it takes to lead with courage and compassion even through the toughest junctures. That willingness to examine yourself honestly and strive to be better is in itself an act of true leadership.

As we both know firsthand, leadership is very demanding. It tests your character and your limits. It tests your very faith in yourself. I have shared my personal stories of success and failure in these pages as witness to the fears, challenges, and regrets every leader faces. I need you to know that you're not alone on this rollercoaster ride. I wrote *The Juncture Code* to help you navigate the twists and turns, and ups and downs. There is only one constant in life and leadership: both are filled with junctures.

As promised in the Introduction, we have explored three big movements across the sixteen chapters in this book:

Understanding How You and Your Brain Work: We've delved into your brain, your emotions, your stress, your sleep, your motivation, your biases, and the social forces that shape how you show up for yourself and your team.

Learning The Juncture Code: We've taken a deep dive in the steps of the Code, so you have a clear, structured framework to bring order, integrity, and courage to all your leadership decisions.

Designing Your Personal Code: We've translated that framework into a dynamic model that fits your unique values, goals, and realities.

Hopefully, at the end of each chapter, you were able to take action after reading the Key Takeaways and Case Studies and participating in the Reflections, Self-Audits, and Exercises. Now that you understand the Juncture Code and how to customize it, the future is yours to create. You've seen that:

- Self-awareness is not indulgent; it's the starting point for responsible decision-making.

- Emotions are not the enemy; unmanaged emotions are.

- Bias is not a moral flaw; unexamined bias is.

- Feedback, vulnerability, and reflection are not optional nice-to-haves; they are critical catalysts.

- A framework without a code is abstract; a code without a framework is unstable. Together, they give you both direction and traction.

If you have your own version of the Juncture Code sketched out on paper, in your head, or in your heart, you've taken a big step. So, what comes next? Going forward, I hope your code enables you to:

Choose courage over autopilot. There will be days when it feels easier to ignore your Code and return to your familiar behaviors. When your calendar is packed, your inbox is overflowing, and the pressure is rising, you'll be tempted to regress. Don't! In those moments, your Code might feel like extra work, but this is exactly when the Code matters most. Pause. Breathe. Reflect. Ask a better question. Challenge a key assumption. Take one more beat before responding. Use your Code! These are the moments when leaders are made—in the small, intentional choices of a stressful day.

Humanize your leadership. Remember that the people you lead live at their own junctures, too. They carry invisible burdens like family crises, financial worries, health struggles, and private doubts into daily meetings and projects. Use your Code not just to decide what to do, but how to do it. Hopefully, this will be with empathy, clarity, and respect. Always ask more questions. Listen longer. Share your own stories, when helpful. Leadership is not simply about making sound decisions; it's about making decisions in a way that honors the people impacted by those decisions.

Treat our Code as a conversation, not a monument. Your life will change. Your personal and professional roles will change. Your organization will change. Some of your current practices will no longer fit two years from now, and that's a good sign. It means you're growing. So, revisit your code regularly. Bring it into team discussions. Invite others to react to it and challenge it. Help your team members build their own Codes. Over time, you may find that the Juncture Code stops being your framework and becomes part of your team's DNA. It becomes your team's way of deciding things. That's how cultures shift from individuals who are willing to go first and lead, to those who follow that lead because what they are experiencing is full of courage, integrity, transparency, and trust.

Before you close this book, I have one last exercise. Take a blank page and write a short letter to your future self. Date it one year from today and answer these three questions:

1. When I look back on this year, even during the most challenging junctures, what kind of leader will I describe?

2. Which part of my personal Code do I most want to strengthen or live more consistently?

3. What will I regret if I don't grow as a leader and what will make me proud of myself as a leader?

Now, seal that letter and put a reminder on your calendar to open it in twelve months. Do it every year and let that future moment become a built-in juncture where you pause, reflect, and decide again who you are intentionally becoming as a leader. In the end, this is the leadership journey. It's not about perfection or never making mistakes. It's not about always knowing the answer. It is about refusing to drift through the decisions that define your life and leadership. It is about meeting your junctures with more honesty, courage, alignment,

   DAVID L ZIMMERMAN, MSC, CPC

and intention. Do this not only for yourself, but all the people who rely on you to do the right thing. The Juncture Code is here to guide you; your personal Code is what will ground you. The rest is your story to write. Thank you for letting me be part of it.

—David "Z"

FOR MORE RESOURCES, TESTIMONIALS, AND
SPEAKING EVENTS, PLEASE VISIT MY WEBSITE.

ABOUT THE AUTHOR

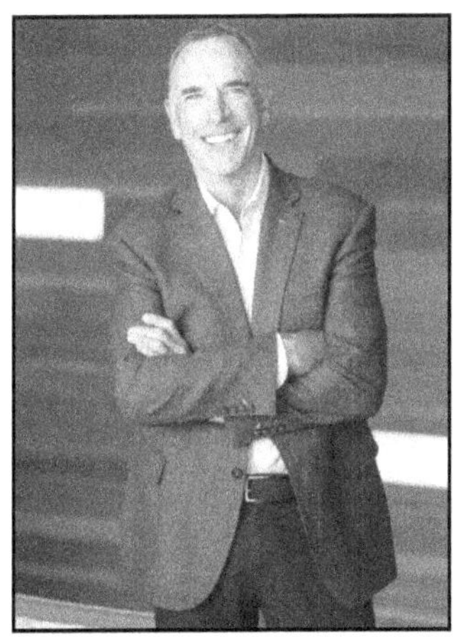**David L. Zimmerman, MSc, CPC**, is a seasoned leadership strategist and executive coach who has spent over 40 years navigating the highest levels of the financial services industry. His journey began in the "trenches" as a financial advisor at EF Hutton and ascended to the C-suite, where he served as CEO and President of First Citizens Bank's broker-dealer and led wealth management divisions for Atlantic Union Bank and Wells Fargo Private Bank.

Throughout his career, David has been a catalyst for growth, leading advanced advisor development at Shearson Lehman Brothers and pioneering the "Client-Valued Business Management" program—a paradigm-shifting framework for business transformation. Today, as the founder of AMAXXA LLC and The Advisor Project LLC, he bridges the gap between deep institutional experience and academic rigor to help leaders design bold strategies and achieve sustainable outcomes in a rapidly changing world.

A Master of Science in Leadership and Executive Coaching and a Certified Professional Coach, David wrote *The Juncture Code* to distill decades of high-stakes decision-making into a practical playbook for the next generation of leaders. He is dedicated to empowering professionals to move past traditional change management and embrace adaptability as their ultimate competitive advantage. David lives in North Carolina, where he continues to mentor leaders and explore the intersection of human potential and organizational success.

     DAVID L ZIMMERMAN, MSC, CPC